BERLITZ®

CALIFORNIA

By the staff of Berlitz Guides

12th edition (1992/1993)

Printed in Switzerland by Weber S.A., Bienne.

How to use our guide

- All the practical information, hints and tips you will need before and during the trip start on p. 103

- For general background, see the sections California and the Californians, p. 6 and A Brief History, p. 14.

- All the sights to see are listed between pp. 29 and 83. Our own choice of sights most highly recommended is pin-pointed by the Berlitz traveller symbol.

- Entertainment, nightlife and other leisure activities are described between pp. 83 and 94, while information on restaurants and cuisine is to be found on pp. 94 to 101.

- Finally, there is an index at the back of the book, pp. 127-128.

Although we make every effort to ensure the accuracy of all the information in this book, changes occur incessantly. We cannot therefore take responsibility for facts, prices, addresses and circumstances in general that are constantly subject to alteration. Our guides are updated on a regular basis as we reprint, and we are always grateful to readers who let us know of any errors, changes or serious omissions they come across.

Text: Jack Altman
Photography: Claude Huber
Layout: Doris Haldemann
We are particularly grateful to Kit Fuller for her help in the preparation of this book. We would also like to thank the San Francisco and Los Angeles Visitor Information Bureaus, and the National Park Service for their valuable assistance.
Cartography: Falk-Verlag, Hamburg.

Contents

Cover picture: Golden Gate Bridge

California and the Californians

European dreamers go to America. American dreamers go to California. A land blessed with sun and sea and oranges and ice-cream, California is quite simply the ultimate fantasy land. As far west as western man can go without starting to go east. Stand on the beach at Malibu, stare out at the Pacific or back at the Santa Monica mountains and everything seems possible: balmy winters, shining summers, snow if you want it.

It's no accident that this is the chosen home of America's cinema. California offers every imaginable landscape for any story, any dream you're likely to imagine—Swiss Alps, Sahara desert, English meadows, African jungle, it's all just a few miles from the freeway. And what isn't already there—a Roman forum or Egyptian pyramid—can be built in a few days with the great wealth that California has amassed in a civilized history of little more than a century. When newspaper baron William Randolph Hearst wanted a Spanish monastery or oil magnate J. Paul Getty a collection of fine art, they had them crated up in Europe and shipped over express.

There are some who feel it's not too pretentious to claim that California is, for better or for worse, the very apex of human evolution. For the last couple of million years, this is where we've been heading. Man, they say, has evolved from hunting through agriculture to industry and on to post-industrial leisure, coping with life so successfully that he can finally enjoy a life of ease and serenity—in California.

Which is not to say that California is a place where people idle the time away. The energy and activity in the state are enormous. Its prosperity is truly overwhelming, and constantly renewed—beginning with the gold of the Sierras, spreading across the great Central Valley to the gigantic combines of agri-business (mere agriculture was just a passing phase), and on to the coast for oil and the aero-space industry. Californians are perfectly prepared to work and work hard, but they can't wait to get back to the tennis court or swimming pool, go surfing in the Pacific or hiking in Yosemite. Life here can be so much fun, it's positively exhausting. After a couple of weeks, you'll be

Powell Street is a great focus of the zip and zest of San Francisco.

almost glad to get back to a spell of homespun humdrum.

Not every Californian is 21 and made of solid bronze with golden hair and blue eyes, standing four inches taller than other people; but sometimes it looks like that.* This is not a place for fogeys. There are some, but they're young in spirit. Youth is king. And it exults in novelty.

In constant quest of the new, in clothes, music, ideas, toys, religions, the people cling to their joyously accepted role as America's last pioneers. Hula-hoop, skate-board, wind-surfing, roller-disco—it all starts, flourishes and fizzles out in California, while the rest of the world takes note and, more often than not, follows suit. Tough-as-iron blue jeans began life in San Francisco to withstand the wear and tear of the 1849 Gold Rush and then became the universal unisex clothing of the last half of

---

*The 19th-century biologist David Starr Jordan wrote: "California college girls are larger by almost every dimension than are the college girls of Massachusetts. They are taller, broader-shouldered, thicker-chested (with ten cubic inches more lung capacity), have larger biceps and calves, and a superiority of tested strength."

our century. Flimsy-as-gossamer bikinis made their first appearance on the beaches of Southern California to attract as much sun and attention as possible. With a few modifications and abbreviations, their principle of merry exhibitionism has survived.

California might not have invented the car, but it was the first place to adopt it as a way of life. Los Angeles not only had the first filling-station but also gave birth to the supermarket, the car's own grocery-store where customers could at last take away more than they could carry. There followed, as a matter of course, the drive-in cine-

California is fun in the park and grace and prosperity in the city.

ma, drive-in restaurant, drive-in bank, drive-in church, and even the drive-in funeral parlour (where you drive up to view your dearly departed behind a special display-window). Since sleep-in vans became popular at the end of the seventies, it's possible to live in California without ever leaving your vehicle. Rumour even has it that some years ago a Los Angeles car-dealer was buried in his Cadillac. **9**

With a population of about 28 million, America's third-largest state has the highest vehicle-inhabitant ratio in the world—two motorcars for every three Californians. The state's expressway system is endless. When you're trying to get to a place, the intricate combination of "freeways", as Californians prefer to call them, is as pervasive a topic of conversation as weather in England or food in France.

But it would be wrong to conclude from this that Californians are inordinately materialistic. If anything, there is a quite pronounced obsession with spirituality. Every imaginable denomination and sect of Christianity, "Jews for Jesus", as well as a variety of esoteric cults, Moonies, scientologists and myriad variations of the ancient faiths of Asia abound. And when they tire of borrowing and adapting from other faiths, the Californians have not hesitated to replace them with their own inventions. "Esalen", "EST" and other self-improvement organizations are listed in the Yellow Pages under "Human Potential Movements".

Despite all that, California is a remarkably conservative state. It welcomes new ideas, but by and large it prefers the old; the majority remain conventional

Christians, conventional Jews, conventional atheists.

Ethnically, the mix is predominantly Anglo-Saxon, but Mexicans are prominent in Los Angeles, Italians and Irish in San Francisco, Jews in both towns. It's only since World War II that blacks have moved to California in appreciable numbers—mostly in the larger cities. The Japanese and Chinese have their most thriving communities in San Francisco, and in recent years

large numbers of immigrants from Korea, Vietnam and Hong Kong have further increased California's Asian population. The original inhabitants, the Indians, now number about 198,000, more than two-thirds of those inhabiting the region when the first Spanish settlers arrived in 1769.

The most enthusiastic tourists in California are Californians. If you want to know where to go, follow the locals. Nobody is more appreciative than they are of the state's natural beauty. In addition to the attraction of California's economic prosperity, people moved here because of the beaches, the mountains, the

Along the wind coast of Big Sur you can face the glory of the Pacific Ocean in solitary meditation, like the first Spanish Conquistadores.

CALIFORNIA

forests and the lakes. San Francisco's steep hills, cramped housing and constant threat of earthquake have done nothing to diminish the appeal of the astounding natural beauty of its location.

The valleys to the north provide delightful wines; to the east and south abundant fruit, vegetables and grain. The Sierra Nevada mountains are a naturalist's paradise, at the heart of which lies Yosemite National Park. The soaring redwood groves of the Sequoia and Kings Canyon National Parks offer a peace where freeways are quickly forgotten. Variegated desert landscapes encourage an inspiring and even invigorating meditation that quickly disperses any foreboding prompted by the name of Death Valley.

Going south from San Francisco, the Pacific coast reveals a thrillingly, adventurously rugged landscape for explorers. Past the stupendous excesses of Hearst's San Simeon castle and down to the sleepy sybaritic beaches of Malibu and suddenly you're in Los Angeles. It's show-time, folks.

And the adventure continues down to the Mexican border. Take a train, take a bus, take a car, take a plane, whichever way you take it, California's a moving daydream.

13

A Brief History

All in all, life in California was easy before the Europeans came. Ever since, for over 400 years, the Spanish and their American successors have struggled with the complications of civilization trying to get back to the leisurely life that seems so natural to the Californian climate and geography.

For the Indians, isolated by ocean, mountains and desert, there had been no urgent need to progress beyond the Stone Age level of culture. They could hunt deer, rabbits and birds, fish for salmon in the rivers and shellfish in the sea, and gather the plentiful fruit, vegetables and nuts. Only along the Colorado River, did they dabble in a little agriculture. Food was in sufficient abundance for them to avoid the warfare that plagued tribes elsewhere in the Americas.

For the most part, Californian Indian tribes lived in harmony with nature. Large numbers of ceremonies and rites were observed to placate the spirits. And anticipating modern misuse of drugs, some tribes drank the juice of the jimson-weed to induce hallucinations—for spiritual reasons, of course.

Then the Spanish arrived, the first of a succession of waves of immigrants.

The Spanish Missions

The first European explorers had landed on the Californian coast in the 16th century but found it more trouble than it was worth. Juan Rodríguez Cabrillo took a look in 1542, located what are now San Diego and Santa Monica and sailed on through the Santa Barbara Channel. He and his followers suffered from scurvy and sea-sickness but found no sign of gold, so they gave up.

England's Francis Drake, on the round-the-world trip that made him a "Sir", stopped off in 1579 at Point Reyes (Drake's Bay just north of San Francisco), and proclaimed the whole coastal territory "New Albion". But the English never went back to settle it.

In the 17th century the Spanish continued to look for a foothold on the California coast as a port of call for their galleon trade returning to Mexico from Manila. They tried Monterey Bay, but abandoned it for lack of shelter. It wasn't until 1769 that missionaries began serious work in California. Their plan was to convert the Indians to Christianity, teach them European farming techniques and other skills and crafts, and then give the land back to them before moving on to set up another mission.

Lompoc Mission—one of the 21 settlements set up to convert and educate the Indians of California.

In fact, the missionaries, at first Jesuits and then Franciscans, remained in place for a century or more, managing and administering the large estates. The Spanish set up 21 missions from San Diego north to Sonoma, with Monterey founded in 1770 as capital of Alta (Upper) California. Baja (Lower) California remained separate and ultimately became Mexican.

The early missionaries, led by Father Junipero Serra, were tough and courageous in the face of great hardships and food-shortages when their first agricultural efforts failed. Some of the more devout didn't mind the personal sacrifices. Others, particularly the soldiers, regarded mission life as a punishment. Typically, rape in Mexico carried with it a sentence of spending the rest of one's life as a citizen of California.

In 1776, while the Yankees across the continent were starting their revolution against the British, 193 Spaniards built the Mission Dolores and a military *presidio* (garrison) on the first advantageous natural bay located on this hitherto inhospitable **15**

California coast. They called it San Francisco.

The first towns proper, as opposed to missions or presidios, were established as food-supply bases, one for the north, the Pueblo de San José de Guadalupe, and one for the south, El Pueblo de Nuestra Señora la Reína de los Angeles del Río de Porciúncula. The Town of Our Lady the Queen of the Angels by the River Porciúncula was mercifully shortened to Los Angeles, founded in 1781 with 46 settlers, mostly Indians.

The Spanish intermarried with the Indians because, unlike the British on the East coast, they could not persuade their women to make the trip from Europe. As the missions evolved with the years, the original aims of the missionaries were obscured and abuses became widespread. Much of the craftwork, leatherwork, tile-manufacture, carpentry and mural painting admired today in Indian souvenir shops was originally Spanish-taught.

The Russians made sporadic attempts at colonization in the early 1800s when their fur-traders came down from Alaska to Fort Ross and as far south as San Francisco, but without much enthusiasm. California just wasn't considered very attractive in those days. Finally the Spanish themselves abandoned

the territory, turning their attention to fighting Napoleon at home and leaving California to the Mexicans.

The Mexicans
As far as California was concerned, the Mexican takeover wasn't very bloody. In fact, California's 26 years of rather loose Mexican administration (1822-48) were characterized by a whole series of bloodless revolutions. To add some excitement to a rather soporific existence, families of *norteños* (northerners) and *sureños* (southerners) fought pitched battles just out of cannonball reach of each other, stopping only to retrieve the enemy's ammunition and fire it back again. The families had intermarried a lot and didn't want to run the risk of killing a wife's brother or father. In this way, the governorship at Monterey changed hands 11 times in a period of five years, not counting three governors whom Mexico City had dared to impose and whose authority was completely ignored.

The "fighting" was for control of the property and lands left by the Spanish missionaries after the Indians were shunted away. California turned into a territory with one industry—cattle *ranchos,* for the sale of cowhide and tallow. The old crafts were abandoned, shoes and other goods from California leather being imported from New England while Chile and Peru turned the tallow into soap and candles. The diet was reduced to beef—fresh or dried.

There were horses galore. Foreshadowing the shape of things to come, no one walked.

Mexicans brought a colourful culture to 19th-century California.

You just took a horse to where you wanted to go and turned it loose. You could always pick up another one later on for the return journey. A proverb quoted in 1846 said that no Californian of Spanish blood would do any work that could not be done on horseback.

California was coming into its own as a place of leisure. There were plenty of parties, dancing the *jota*, the *fandango* and the

bamba and the *borrego*. Apart from the cannonball-sprees, the most energetic pastime was the annual *rodeo* cattle round-up for branding the free-roaming calves.

The American Pioneers

The first Americans to come to California from "back East" as they'd say now, were Boston traders in furs and seal and otter skins, taking the Cape Horn route at the end of the 18th century. But they didn't stay. Gradually traders and fur-trappers came overland via Nevada, Arizona and New Mexico, settling only in dribs and drabs until the covered wagons began their heroic treks of the 1840s. The hardships they suffered in the Sierra Nevada mountains and the Mojave desert became the stuff of California legend, the most tragic being the fate of 87 pioneers who set out from Illinois in 1846. George Donner's wagon train was snowed in from November to February high in the Sierras north of Lake Tahoe at a point now known as Donner Pass. Only 47 survived and then only by eating their dead.

These pioneers, simple farmers seeking a place in the sun to work a piece of land, came at a time when territorial expansion was much in vogue—the French in the Pacific and Algeria, the British in Africa and the Far East, and the United States eager to get in on the act. During their war with Mexico over the annexation of Texas, California was suddenly regarded as a useful addition to the spoils. In 1845 President James Polk approved a campaign of conquest at the urging of a brash, pushy adventurer named John Fremont, on the totally unfounded, but enormously persuasive, argument that if the U.S. did not take California, Britain would.

The war-weary Mexicans saw themselves hopelessly outnumbered although they did win a couple of honourable victories near San Diego and Los Angeles —battles fought in response to the overbearing behaviour of occupying American forces rather than any deep desire to hold on to California. The U.S. forces recaptured Los Angeles in 1847 and the Mexicans capitulated at Cahuenga. A treaty of American annexation of California was signed on February 2, 1848. Meanwhile, unknown to the American and Mexican signatories, gold had been discovered in the Sierra Nevada foothills nine days earlier.

The Gold Rush

Actually, ranchero Francisco Lopez had found California's first recorded gold in 1842, when he pulled up some wild onions at Placerita Creek, north-west of Los Angeles, and found gold particles sticking to the roots. But nobody paid attention.

The find that started all the fuss—two thousand million dollars' worth over the next century—was made at the sawmill of John Sutter, a Swiss immigrant. Carpenter James Wilson Marshall was digging a tailrace for the mill, on the American River at Coloma, midway between Sacramento and Lake Tahoe. He found 23-carat gold particles in the river's silt and this time people took notice. That first year (1848) there were 6,000 seekers from Hawaii, Oregon, Utah, Mexico, Peru and Chile, who found $10 million worth of gold. In 1849 the real mad Gold Rush began (San Francisco's football team today is known as the '49-ers), with 40,000 fortune-hunters from all over North and South America scrabbling for $30 million worth of gold. By 1852, there were 100,000 miners in the region, all fiercely individualistic, working at their personal, private stakes rather than banding together in industrialized mining.

An editorial in the *San Francisco Californian* railed against the "sordid cry of gold, GOLD, GOLD! while the field is half-planted, the house half-built and everything neglected but the manufacture of shovels and pick-axes". Then the newspaper suspended publication so that the staff could go off and join the rush.

For those whose backs were too weak to dig for gold, there was another fortune to be made from the side-industries and San Francisco, home of the first banks and manufacturers of mining equipment, began its growth into a metropolis. The first gadgets for mining were mostly useless but nonetheless profitable for their makers. More lasting in value were the strong trousers which entrepreneur Levi Strauss made first from tent canvas and a tough twill-weave known as "denim jean". Manuals such as *The Emigrant's Guide to the Gold Mines* became instant best-sellers, 30 pages for 25 cents, half price without the map—which was a better bargain because the map was completely wrong. The sheet music best-seller list was full of such tunes as "The Gold Digger's Waltz" and "The Sacramento Gallop".

Lured by the promise of increased federal revenues from the discovery of gold, the U.S. Congress gave California rapid admission to the Union, in 1850, with the status of a fully fledged state rather than the usual interim status of "territory". **19**

In the middle of nowhere, a ghost-town waits for the next Gold Rush.

Statehood

The early years of statehood were full of rough and tumble. In the absence of a well-established judiciary and an organized police force, law and order—or rather lynch-law—was enforced by vigilante groups such as the San Francisco Committee of Vigilance made up of the town's leading businessmen. Instant hanging was the usual punishment as the vigilantes had no prisons.

Life was not easy for Mexicans, Chinese and Indians. The Mexicans, 15,000 strong at California's accession to statehood, were excluded from mining by being subjected to a heavy "foreigner's" tax. Two-thirds of them were forced to leave. The Chinese arrived in the wake of the great Taiping Rebellion of 1851, seeking security and prosperity in what they'd been told were California's "Golden Mountains". They suffered both exploitation by Chinese entrepreneurs, who used them as indentured labour, and discriminatory taxation by the state legis-

lature. But the worst treated were the Indians, whose numbers dwindled from 275,000 in 1769 to 30,000 by 1870, mostly through disease, starvation and malnutrition, but also by being subjected to systematic massacres in the 1850s by California militia such as the Mariposa Battalion that hunted down the Yosemites and Chowchillas. The Indians had originally been promised 8,619,000 acres of land, but the state legislature then objected that the land was worth $100 million in gold-bearing quartz and so they ended up with 624,000 acres of largely worthless land. (Worthless at the time. Ironically, it included the desert of Palm Springs, now transformed into a millionaire's paradise east of Los Angeles.)

Meanwhile, in 1859, the discovery of silver (the Comstock Lode in western Nevada) caused a Silver Rush in the reverse direction, with the mining being organized almost completely from California. With the growth of the state's economy, the major priority became a railway to connect the state to the Eastern markets.

The building of the railway was a saga of ingenuity, courage **21** and the breathtaking ruthlessness of entrepreneurial capitalism. Engineer Theodore Judah defied all the Eastern experts by plotting a railway link between Sacramento and the East, passing right through the Sierra Nevada and the Rocky Mountains. He sold the idea to a San Francisco consortium that became known as the Central Pacific's "Big

The Chinese toiled on the railway for a piece of the American cake.

Four"—Mark Hopkins, Collis Huntington, Leland Stanford and Charles Crocker—names that still resound today. They parlayed their combined personal assets of $100,000 in 1861 into a fortune of $200 million through exploitation of the railroad. The line, linking up with the Union Pacific at Promontory, Utah, in 1869, was built under the most hazardous conditions, using cheap Chinese labour. The coolies, as they were known, often worked suspended in wicker baskets over sheer mountain cliffs to hammer and chisel a ledge around the Sierras.

The Great Earthquake

The more devout Californians were convinced God was punishing San Francisco's gold-lust and sinfulness when an earthquake, registering 8.25 on the Richter Scale, struck the city at 5.14 a.m. on Wednesday, April 18, 1906. The initial tremor wiped out 5,000 homes, but 50 different fires that resulted from the quake destroyed 23,000 more buildings. With the water mains shattered, the City Fire Department was helpless to stop the fires spreading and they raged for three whole days. Federal soldiers from the presidio marched into town to take control and were given dynamite to blow up buildings and prevent the fires

spreading. Unfortunately, none of the military had any real experience with explosives. The wooden shanties of Chinatown had miraculously escaped the flames until the soldiers blew up a nearby drugstore; a burning mattress from an upstairs apartment flew across the road and Chinatown was burned to the ground. This was one of many fires started, rather than stopped, by the explosives.

The earthquake and fires caused 452 deaths, according to official estimates, but the martial law imposed on the town by Mayor Schmitz (without federal authorization) caused up to 100 more deaths in summary executions for real or apparent looting, profiteering or refusing to help fight the fires. The performance of the military was less than exemplary. As Chinatown burned, it was looted by the National Guardsmen sent to protect it from looters.

Reform, Progress and Oil

The San Francisco earthquake helped to focus the nation's attention on the graft and corruption rife throughout California. The federal prosecution succeeded in sending only a few of the principals involved in the rackets to jail, but the publicity was enough to make "reform" a popular concept. **23**

The movement, intent on breaking the political power of the big corporations, attacked corrupt practices in administration, public finances and banking, but did not oppose the businessmen's traditional resistance to unions in agriculture or more liberal labour laws in the big cities. Nor did its "progressive" label mean that reformist governor, Hiram Johnson, could not get repeatedly re-elected in a campaign for laws against "the yellow peril", now directed against the Japanese rather than the Chinese.

Quite apart from being very much in keeping with the nationalism of the times, these discriminatory practices were perhaps inevitable in a young state eager to find and assert its own identity. Its burgeoning prosperity seemed too good to be true. Absolutely everything grew in California, every imaginable fruit, vegetable and grain. People didn't become farmers, they became specialized producers of oranges, tomatoes, lettuces, avocados, all a little bigger and brighter-coloured than elsewhere. But the most profitable thing to come from the Californian earth was oil.

Drilling had begun in the 1860s, but didn't get anywhere until 1892, when Edward Doheny took a walk in Los Angeles past some workmen carting "greasy brown dirt" away from the corner of West Second Street and Glendale Boulevard. Lawyer Doheny looked at the grease and found it was oil. By the 1920s, Standard, Union and Shell oil companies had their derricks all over the Los Angeles basin. In that one decade, the state's oil revenues were $2,500 million, $500 million more than all the gold that the Sierras produced in a century.

In a city spreading across an oil-spouting desert, Los Angeles was the perfect place for the car to emerge as an everyday household tool. From 1920 to 1930, L.A. more than doubled its population to 2,208,492 and private cars quintupled to 806,264. Noting the central position of the "pursuit of happiness" in America's Declaration of Independence, the *Los Angeles Times* asked in 1926 "how can one pursue happiness by any swifter and surer means than by the use of the automobile?"

Hollywood

If you didn't feel like pursuing happiness in a car, you could always sit in the dark and dream about happiness in the cinema. Again, California was the place that made it happen. First of all because of its distance from New York and Thomas Edison's lawyers seeking to stop film-makers from pirating the great man's invention. William Selig was the first to go West, dodging Edison's process-servers by sending a film-crew in 1907 to shoot *The Count of Monte Cristo* in a studio on Main Street, Los Angeles. One company tried the San Francisco Bay area, making 375 cowboy films in six years—

Marilyn, Groucho, Clark, James and Rudolph, a few favourite idols from California's dream factory.

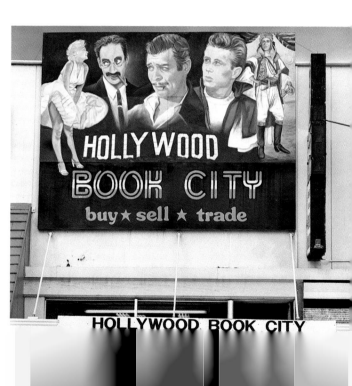

HOLLYWOOD BOOK CITY
buy ★ sell ★ trade

HOLLYWOOD BOOK CITY

more than one a week—but the filmmakers finally preferred a little suburb of Los Angeles named Hollywood.

There were lots of reasons: the producers liked the closeness to the Mexican border, across which cameras, equipment and filmstock could be driven out of the clutches of patent-holding confiscators; at a time when artificial lighting was insufficient for cameras to function indoors, the cameramen liked southern California's guaranteed year-round good light conditions; the director could duplicate the Mediterranean, Africa, Asia or whatever, without driving more than half an hour out of town; and the financiers liked the looser labour laws and lower taxes, compared with New York.

Hollywood became a mecca for society's down-and-outs. Dubious "talent schools" sprouted for small-town girls hoping to emulate film stars like Mary Pickford and if they didn't become actresses the school turned them into callgirls for the producers. In 1922, the lurid rape trial of comic Fatty Arbuckle highlighted Hollywood's decadent life of fast cars, bootleg whisky and drugs. The immediate reaction was the Hays Office code of morals which laid down that in all Hollywood films sin must be punished—it could be

Cinema architecture–art at the service of industry.

shown in detail, but it must be punished.

The industry—Hollywood always thought of cinema first as an industry and only second as an art—cashed in on the boom years of the 1920s. Hollywood Boulevard introduced lavish exotic Egyptian- or Chinese-style cinemas that looked like sets from the more spectacular extravaganzas being shown inside. And the film stars had homes to match in Beverly Hills, the most famous being "Pickfair", a hunting lodge which Mary Pickford and Douglas Fairbanks turned into a honeymoon estate. But the glamour didn't overcome the immoral image. Boarding houses in Los Angeles sometimes advertised: "Rooms for rent—no dogs or actors allowed."

Depression and Boom

The Great Depression hit California hard. Farm income dropped 50 per cent between 1929 and 1932 and 1,250,000 people were on public relief—one-fifth of the state's population. The hard times encouraged California's natural inclination for evangelistic, social and spiritual movements. One of the most successful was Sister Aimee Semple McPherson's. Her "Four Square Gospel" on the Los Angeles radio brought her an enormous following until she was found to have spent a weekend with her choir-director in a Carmel motel at a time she claimed she'd been kidnapped and held for ransom. Unemployed businessmen formed an equally fervent society for Technocracy—a word invented in California in 1932—believing only management experts like themselves could save American civilization.

Then came World War II, which brought an enormous boom for the state's beleaguered economy. The federal government spent $35,000 million—10 per cent of the national war budget—in California. Overnight, ships and airplanes became the state's most important products. Douglas, Lockheed, North American and Northrop all located in the Los Angeles area. In case of Japanese air attacks, Douglas built dummy houses, streets and trees to blend its Santa Monica factory into the surrounding residential community.

Post-war California continued its growth and prosperity. Agribusiness became a colossus; the aircraft industry was supplemented by space technology and the cinema industry at first felt threatened by and then happily embraced the new monster of television. The TV networks kept their corporate offices in New York, close to Wall Street, but moved their production centres to Los Angeles, close to the sun.

Beatniks, Hippies and Modern Times

In the now well-established tradition of California's indulgence of utopian dreams, San Francisco's North Beach district in the 1950s was the first home of the existentialist Beat Generation led by writers Jack Kerouac and Allen Ginsberg and the poets that hung around Lawrence Ferlinghetti's City Lights Bookshop. By 1957, in analogy with the just-launched Russian Sputnik, they became popularised by journalists as "beatniks". Ten years later, the press invented the term "hippies" (a diminutive of Norman Mailer's coinage "hipster") for the flower-children that clustered around San Francisco's Haight-Ashbury district. These inhabitants of what Joan Didion called "America's first teenage slum" dispensed a sometimes charming, sometimes confused vision of love, peace and light, heavily laced with marijuana and more dangerous drugs like LSD—an echo of the California when Indians drank jimson-weed juice.

California was also in the forefront of student radicalism, beginning with the Free Speech Movement at Berkeley in 1964 and ending with the violent clashes of San Francisco State College in 1968 and a 1969 Berkeley demonstration for a People's Park where militants were sprayed with teargas from a helicopter.

Black radicalism accelerated after the Watts riots in Los Angeles in 1965 and reached its peak with the Black Panthers in Oakland, a paramilitary group led by Huey Newton, Eldridge Cleaver and Bobby Seale.

America's ongoing social revolution has always had a prominent place in California life. Pressures for change have been alternately encouraged and resisted as the state's volatile political establishment has swung back and forth between conservatives and progressives.

From the Catholic fervour of Father Junipero Serra to the Zen meditation of Governor Jerry Brown the state has spanned a spectrum of ideals and politics that defy any simple categorization. The voters seem to choose state governments that bear no obvious relationship to what's happening in the rest of the country; except perhaps to show what may possibly happen there tomorrow.

Where to Go

Many Californians would like to divide their state into two new states, North and South California—corresponding to what they believe to be two distinct frames of mind represented by San Francisco and Los Angeles. But in fact there's a little bit of both—San Francisco's sophistication and Los Angeles' sunny craziness—all over the place.

Our itinerary begins in San Francisco and its nearby wine valleys and works its way down the Pacific coast to Los Angeles and San Diego before taking off across to the National Parks at Yosemite, Sequoia and Death

In Venice (California) the street frescoes have a lift of their own.

Valley. You can turn this itinerary upside down, but either way, if you have the time, you should also consider an excursion to California's favourite out-of-state playground—Las Vegas.

You can get to almost all these places by train or bus, and air travel is relatively cheap compared with the rest of the country and a great bargain compared with Europe. However, California is inevitably the land of the car and it will be difficult for you to enjoy the full scope of the vast and varied landscape without driving. San Francisco is a walking town, with buses and cable-cars to help you up and down the hills, but Los Angeles is resolutely a driving town (although it is trying to alleviate its congestion and pollution by tunnelling for an underground system, and has inaugurated a commuter railway). Yosemite and Sequoia are splendid for hiking—cars are even discouraged—but Death Valley needs a covered wagon.

San Francisco

San Franciscans are unashamedly in love with their town. All over the place you see the boast: "Everybody's Favorite City". The town's natural setting, nestling in the hills around the bay, make it uncommonly cosy; the zip in the air is invigorating and even the fog rolling off the ocean is romantic rather than chilling. The pervasive enthusiasm of the residents is difficult to resist. Even the earthquake that hit them hard in 1989 couldn't keep their spirits down for long. Just one tip: don't call their town "Frisco". It makes true San Franciscans shudder.

If you have a car, the best way to begin your visit is to take the **49 Mile Scenic Drive,** a comprehensive tour of the main sights that gives you a good overall picture before you start to explore in detail. Stop off at **Twin Peaks,** south of Golden Gate Park, for an excellent panoramic view of the city and its bay.

Then put away the car, put on a pair of good walking shoes and use the city's first-class public transport. Start at the bridge. There are more than one, but *the* bridge is of course the **Golden Gate**. It is, in fact, not golden but a deep burnt sienna or reddish-brown, depending on the light; the masterpiece of engineer Joseph Strauss. At 4,200 feet, it's not the longest, but few would deny it's the most beautiful sus-

Nobody's left on Alcatraz; strike up the band, bring on the clowns!

years to repaint—a job that begins again as soon as it's finished. Take a bus to the entrance of the bridge and walk across; as exciting an urban adventure as climbing the Eiffel Tower or the Empire State Building. The bridge sways beneath your feet and the lamp-posts rattle as the wind whistles through the swooping cables.

While you're here, spare a thought for the **Oakland Bay Bridge** visible in the distance. The silvery bridge swings across

One of the great urban adventures of the Western world—a cable-car.

to Oakland via Yerba Buena island and at 8¼ miles is one of the world's longest. It's the bridge you'll take to Berkeley.

South of the Golden Gate Bridge is the **Presidio,** site of the original garrison built by the Spanish to protect their settlement in 1776. It is now the headquarters of the Sixth Army and remarkably green and pretty for a military establishment.

architecture and the reinforced-concrete "Roman ruin" outside contrast with the modern technological wizardry that it houses in its Exploratorium museum—holography, lasers, solar-operated musical instruments—great for the kids on a rainy day.

From the western Yacht Harbor you can make your way along Marina Boulevard, past its fine waterfront houses, to **Fisherman's Wharf.** Geared more to tourism than fishing these days, the area offers attractions as diverse as a wax museum and Guinness Museum of World Records. Seafood stands line the wharf—though the fish may well be imported—and there are two shopping-centres, Ghirardelli Square, a converted old red-brick chocolate factory, and The Cannery, once a fruit-processing plant. Directly east of Fisherman's Wharf is the popular **Pier 39**, another large complex of restaurants, shops and entertainments. Visitors are rewarded with spectacular views of the bay, Alcatraz and the Golden Gate Bridge.

On your way down to the Yacht Harbor, you'll pass the **Palace of Fine Arts,** a weird rebuilt relic (the original was chicken-wire and plaster) from the 1915 Panama-Pacific Exposition. Its hodgepodge of classical

---

The Cable Caper

If you think the cable car is just a tourist gimmick, how do you explain why there are always so many native San Franciscans aboard? It's clearly one of the most enjoyable rides you can imagine. Especially standing on the outside step—dangerous but legal, like so many things in this city—hanging on for your life as the Powell Street car clangs up and down Nob Hill.

The Hills

There are 40 of them, and they're San Francisco's pride and challenge but you don't have to tackle them all. A tour of Nob Hill (Powell or California Street cable-car), Telegraph Hill (bus) and Russian Hill (cable-car) will give you a good sense of the past and present splendours of San Francisco's wealthy, many of whom have preferred to stay in the city at a time when many prosperous citizens have moved out to the suburbs.

The cable cars were first installed in 1873 and one of the originals can still be seen in the museum, which is also the system's fascinating working centre at Washington and Mason. The hand-made cars are constantly being refurbished and overhauled, so don't be surprised if one or another of the cable-lines is not functioning. By the way, you're not allowed on with an ice-cream, because the bone-shaking ride would almost certainly land it on the lap of a fellow passenger.

The monumental Victorian houses of **Nob Hill**—just as its name suggests, home of the "nobs" or nabobs—were wiped out in the 1906 earthquake (see p. 23) and only the imposing brown-stone house of James Flood, now the highly exclusive Pacific Union Club, survived.

You can't get in there, but you can loiter (with appropriate decorum) in the two landmark hotels on the hill, the Fairmont and the Mark Hopkins. A drink in their panoramic bars in the Crown Room or the Top of the Mark is worth the stiff price for the view.

Grace Cathedral, at the corner of California and Jones, is not an especially happy neo-Gothic effort, but worth a look in passing for a remarkable example of San Francisco's continuing romance with Europe in its Ghiberti doors—bronze reproductions of the Baptistry East Doors in Florence. You may also be impressed by the 12 stained-glass windows dedicated to "Human Endeavor" and depicting, among others, Albert Einstein, Franklin D. Roosevelt, Frank Lloyd Wright and Henry Ford—saints for our century?

Telegraph Hill is best climbed for its view of the other hills from the top of Coit Tower, built in 1934 to honour the city's fire-department. Its shape is meant to resemble the nozzle of a fire-hose.

Russian Hill's opulence is less obvious than the other two, but its gardens and immaculate little cottages make it more appealing. The constant dips and climbs of the hills, breaking the monotony of the standard American urban grid-system of streets, reaches its crazy climax on **Lombard Street** between Hyde and Leavenworth. After you've negotiated the breakneck serpentine plunge in and out of gardens of hydrangeas and lilac around seven sudden bends, you're not going to quibble about the claim that it's the "crookedest street in the world."

Downtown

North Beach is not a beach. It's the district north of the intersection of Broadway and Columbus that is both centre of the Italian community and focus of the city's artistic, intellectual and cosmopolitan life. Before the earthquake fires burned most of it down, part of it was known as the Barbary Coast, where sailors came for the brothels while their captains shanghaied drunken and otherwise unconscious civilians out to their ships to complete the crew.

From the days when poet Lawrence Ferlinghetti gathered his fellow beatniks around his City Lights Bookshop in the 1950s (see p. 27), North Beach has been the place where California's new ideas, intellectual and other, are first tried out.

The children's nursery has taken over this house on Russian Hill.

SAN FRANCISCO DOWNTOWN

The few relatively literate hippies of the sixties congregated here to escape the mindless nonsense of Haight-Ashbury (at the eastern edge of Golden Gate Park). In the seventies it was the turn of the "mellows", the smiling younger brothers and sisters of the hippies, gliding around on quiet roller-skates, eating frozen yoghurt and espousing low-risk ecological causes. Whatever trend emerges in the future, a couple of Grant Avenue coffee shops have survived to offer you ringside seats to watch it all begin. On sunny days, picnic on Washington Square.

Chinese newcomers are making inroads into this Little Italy of cafés, grocery stores, ice-cream parlours and bookstores, clustered around Columbus, Stockton, Vallejo and Green Street. The seedy tradition of the Barbary Coast lives on in the dwindling "topless" and "bottomless" joints—San Francisco's gifts to the Western world—on Broadway. Here you'll also find some fine jazz nightclubs and opera-cafés where amateurs sing arias remarkably well.

Chinatown has evolved from a ghetto imposed on the Chinese in the 19th century by the founders of the city, into a proud self-assertive community that has won the town's admiration. Gone are the Tong wars for the control of the community's underworld around the opium dens. The vicarious thrill that those adventures provided has now been replaced by a general civic pride, though Chinatown's elders show some concern for the future: rising rents are driving out small family businesses and the upwardly-mobile continue their exodus to suburbs.

There are more than 82,000 Chinese in the city, making it the largest Chinese community outside Asia. The main neighbourhood is bounded by Broadway, Bush, Kearny and Stockton, with eight blocks of Grant Avenue being its colourful centre.

At the Bush Street end of Grant, you enter through the ornamental Chinatown Gateway arch. Flanking it are two hamburger houses of Chinese design. Inside Chinatown proper the life is more resolutely Chinese. The restaurants, grocery, porcelain and silk shops have an English translation alongside their Chinese signs for the tourists, but the banks, travel agencies and law offices don't always make the same concession. Not that you won't see the influence of the surrounding American culture in such institutions as the Catholic St. Mary's Chinese School at Clay and Stockton or the neo-Gothic Old St. Mary's Church.

After you've finished your shopping on Grant Avenue, start exploring the side streets—Spofford, Ross, Waverly and Wentworth, for example—among the garment workshops, porcelain warehouses and fortune-cookie factories.

On a smaller scale, but with the same cultural pride is **Japan Town**—known as J-Town to San Franciscans. Its Cultural and Trade Center at Geary between Laguna and Fillmore includes a cookery school, florists teaching Japanese flower-arrangement and a hotel with Japanese amenities—sunken Japanese bathtubs, mattresses on *tatami* mats, kimonoed maids and a landscaped garden outside the window.

After which you might want to remind yourself of America's dominant culture, the Anglo-Saxon variety downtown. Drive down Market Street, the city's main thoroughfare (walking is best avoided to be on the safe side), until you reach the wedge formed with Van Ness Street. Here you will find a sprawling complex of municipal, state and federal buildings, known collectively as the **Civic Center.** It was initiated in an ambitious burst of city planning after the 1906 earthquake, and the early structures—note especially the gold-domed City Hall and the handsome Main Public Library—are in Renaissance style. Also part of the complex are the twin Veterans' Building (housing the San Francisco Museum of Modern Art) and Opera House, where the United Nations Charter was signed in 1945.

Turn off Market at Powell Street for a shopping detour. **Union Square** is the place to go for fashionable boutiques, speciality shops, flower stands and large department stores. Continue on to Montgomery Street, the heart of San Francisco's financial district, also known as the "Wall Street of the West". Here, in the home of the Gold Rush heirs, take a look at the **Old Coin and Gold Exhibit** of the Bank of California (400 California Street). You're not likely to miss the **Transamerica Pyramid,** an 853-foot spike at the corner of Montgomery and Washington streets. It's one of those buildings that purists start off hating for its clash with the "spirit" of San Francisco and then defend in the next generation as an epitome of its age.

Golden Gate Park

Away from the skyscrapers of downtown, take the number 5

Wall paintings proliferate in California; even in Chinatown.

Fulton bus to get to Golden Gate Park. Originally a wasteland of sand dunes, it was turned into its present lush parkland quite by chance when 19th-century urban planner John McLaren accidentally dropped the oats from his horse's nosebag and came back later to find the oats had sprouted.

Now it is a delightful landscape of small lakes and hills, arboretum and botanical gardens, baseball diamonds, soccer fields, riding stables with polo grounds, and a popular open-air chess hangout known paradoxically as the Card Shelter. At the eastern end of the park there's a superb children's playground and beyond it, the Haight-Ashbury district of the 1960s' "flower children". Although it is still a somewhat depressed area, a regular infusion of new shops and boutiques, along with steady "gentrification" by eighties' yuppies, promises continued improvement.

Situated in the park are three major museums, clustered around the Music Concourse. The **M. H. de Young Memorial Museum** has an impressive selection of works by Titian, Tintoretto, El Greco, Cranach and Rembrandt in its permanent collection. However, it is better known as host to important travelling exhibitions coming to the

West Coast. The **Asian Art Museum** next door has the rich Avery Brundage collection and the **California Academy of Sciences** houses a zoological museum, an aquarium, and a planetarium. The **Japanese Tea Garden** is a good place to rest afterwards.

There's a splendid panorama of the Pacific at the imposing **Palace of the Legion of Honor,** somehow more striking in the middle of the Lincoln Park golf course than the original on Paris's Quai d'Orsay. Inside there's a collection of French art (closed for renovation until the mid-nineties). To enjoy the ocean go down to nearby Ocean Beach.

Joggers in Golden Gate Park; worlds away from topless bars and the Transamerica Pyramid.

Alcatraz

Of the many cruises you can take on San Francisco Bay the most entertaining (from Pier 41, near Fisherman's Wharf) is out to the abandoned prison of Alcatraz. The U.S. Rangers conduct excellent informative and witty guided tours of the old home of Al Capone and fellow convicts too hot for the other prisons to hold. A distortion of the Spanish Isla de los Alcotraces (Isle of Pelicans), it's a 12-acre rock with no arable soil, and all the water for the shrubs and trees there today had to be brought by the U.S. Army, for whom it had been a "disciplinary barracks" until 1934. Separated from the San Francisco shore by 1½ miles of ice-cold, treacherous currents, sharks and raw sewage, it was the ideal location for America's most notorious federal civil penitentiary, but enormously expensive in upkeep. By 1962, with one guard for every three inmates, each prisoner was cost-ing $40,000 a year and Attorney General Robert Kennedy closed it down.

You will see what "maximum security, minimum privilege" meant for Alcatraz's 250 to 300 inmates, each alone in a cell 9 feet by 5 by 7, with three 20-minute periods of recreation each day and two hours on Sundays. They used to lock visitors away in "The Hole" as a gimmick—until one was accidentally incarcerated for hours. "The Hole" meant unlighted solitary confinement for especially difficult prisoners. There were "luxuries"—*hot* showers so that inmates wouldn't get used to cold water and be able to survive the waters of San Francisco Bay; and remarkably good food. One inmate returning for the guided tour—many do, out of nostalgia—said the food was better than he'd eaten in many San Francisco hotels. The prisoners named the cell-rows after elegant American streets such as New

---

Getting Away from it All

Officially, nobody ever got away safely from Alcatraz. In all, 39 tried, seven were killed in the attempt, and five have never been found but are assumed drowned.

In 1962, at the very end of Alcatraz's grim history, John Paul Scott made it unharmed to San Francisco by greasing his body to resist the cold. Some students found him exhausted at Fort Point by the Golden Gate Bridge. Good-naturedly, not knowing he was an escaped prisoner, they called the police to help the poor fellow in his moment of distress.

York's Park Avenue, Los Angeles' Sunset Boulevard and Chicago's Michigan Avenue. Al Capone's cell was on "B" Block, 2nd tier, N° 200.

The Bay Area

Sausalito and Tiburon

Immediately north of San Francisco are the two charming little harbour towns of Sausalito and Tiburon, which you can reach either by car across the Golden Gate Bridge or by ferry (from the Ferry Building for Sausalito or Pier 43½ for Tiburon). With Tiburon the quieter of the two, the towns have a colourful Mediterranean atmosphere (the San Francisco area lends itself to European analogies), with a number of—more or less—tasteful boutiques and pleasant bistros and cafés out

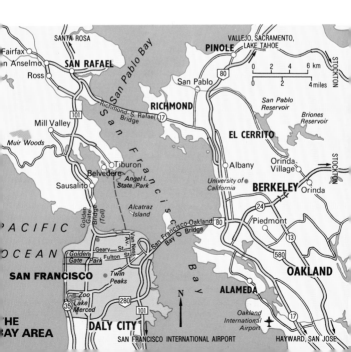

on the boardwalk looking across the bay to San Francisco. Sausalito and Tiburon are at the southern tip of the Californian phenomenon of Marin County, home of the hot tubs, Jacuzzi whirlpool baths and other sensual delights of communal living, spearhead of mellow fellowship. The perpetrators are not freaks, at least not any more, they've grown into lawyers and investment bankers. This, they'll tell you, is where the Good Life begins.

Berkeley
Take the Bay Area Rapid Transit (BART) subway train from Market Street or drive across the Bay Bridge to make your pilgrimage to the campus of Berkeley, the University of California's home of student radicalism in the 1960s. Tours are organized from the Student Union at the end of Telegraph Avenue. The free and easy access to the university's facilities will give you an insight into Berkeley's open "personality". Sneak into the cafeteria and you may be in time for the next revolution.

The Wine Country
Wine-lovers will enjoy a drive through the vineyard of **Napa Valley** and across the Maacama Mountains to Sonoma. Bus-tours are also available and it's a good idea to contact an agency specializing in wine-tours—the San Francisco Visitor's and Convention Bureau in Market Street can provide names. The wineries, as they call themselves, provide tours and tastings in the cellars and organize picnics in the vineyards. Harvests begin around mid-August—Californian weather being so much more predictably sunny than Europe's.

Some of the more interesting wineries are at Sterling, where you visit the vineyard by aerial tramway across the valley, and at Mondavi, Martini, Beaulieu and Beringer in Napa and Souverain and Sebastiani in Sonoma. Homesick Frenchmen may want to visit the Chandon champagne property in Napa. The Hess Collection Winery near Napa exhibits artworks by Stella, Motherwell and some of the ultra-realists. A warning: following French tradition, the best restaurants of the region are closed on Tuesdays.

Drive back from the wine country via **Point Reyes** on the coast, with its beautiful rolling hills and wild surf. Stop at

Lunchtime for a Sausalito houseboat and picnickers on the wharf.

Drake's Bay, a peaceful cove where Sir Francis Drake nearly pinched California from the Spanish in 1579. If you can't manage a visit to the Sequoia National Park, make sure you at least visit the more accessible **Muir Woods,** named after the great Scottish naturalist John Muir, who explored the Sierra Nevada mountains and Californian coast and founded the state's conservation movement at the turn of the 20th century. The best examples of sequoias are at Bohemian Grove.

Pacific Coast

Take Freeway 101 south from San Francisco and join Pacific Highway, Route 1, at Castroville, to get to **Monterey,** the old Spanish and Mexican capital of Alta (Upper) California. The Bay was discovered in 1542 but was not settled until 1770 when Father Junipero Serra set up a mission there with the garrison protection of Gaspar de Portola's presidio. Monterey was a bleak, disease-ridden place and Portola recommended it be handed over to the Russians, who also coveted it, "as a punishment". But Father Serra accepted the hardships and led the taming of the Monterey wilderness. His statue looks down on the bay from Corporal Ewin Road.

The town is proud of its past and offers a sign-posted tour of the Old Town's historic buildings from the 19th-century Mexican administration and early American period. The architecture is a strange mixture of Spanish adobe and American colonial clapboard, two storeys with a balcony; an attractive enough hybrid to earn it the

Windswept trees of Monterey and Carmel provide unforgettable vistas.

name of "Monterey-style". At the Chamber of Commerce, on Alvarado Street, you can get a map showing the major houses.

Look for the **Larkin House** at Jefferson and Calle Principal, home of the first (and only) U.S. Consul in the 1840s, and the **Robert Louis Stevenson House,** 530 Houston Street, where the writer lived while he was working on *Treasure Island*. On Church Street you'll find the site of Father Serra's original baked-mud church; rebuilt in 1795, it's now the **Royal Presidio Chapel** or Cathedral of San Carlos de Borromeo. To the left of the altar is a colourful 18th-century Virgin Mary from Spanish Mexico. Nearer the waterfront are the Pacific House, on Custom House Plaza, with a pleasant arcaded courtyard, and the Custom House (1827) taken over as the first U.S. federal building on the Pacific coast. Casa del Oro, at Scott and Oliver, is said to have been a storehouse for gold.

More distinctively American is **California's First Theater** on Scott and Pacific Streets, a pinewood shack built by one Jack Swan in 1847 as a saloon with a dubious apartment house upstairs. Customers were attracted—and still are—by Victorian melodramas, but the "apartment house" no longer operates.

Monterey's **Fisherman's Wharf,** like San Francisco's, is a collection of shops and restaurants out on the dock, but offering a more intimate view across the boats of the marina. The fish here are most definitely fresh. But not abundant enough to keep Cannery Row going as more than a weather-beaten curiosity. Its sardine-fisheries closed down in the 1940s—for lack of sardines—but the timbered canneries made famous by novelist John Steinbeck as "a poem, a stink, a grating noise", keep going today as cosy little boutiques and artists' studios.

A draw in the neighbourhood, the **Monterey Bay Aquarium** features the denizens of the bay. The vast main tank contains a kelp forest three stories high, home of many of the 500-plus species on display.

Take the **17 Mile Drive** starting at Lighthouse Avenue in PACIFIC GROVE through some beautiful cypress groves along a rocky coastline where you can fish for abalone, go crabbing and skin-diving. The famous Pebble Beach golf courses go down to the water's edge, as do many of the luxurious mansions.

The 17 Mile Drive takes you down to the delightful resort town of **Carmel,** ideal for a rest, a suntan and some serious shopping if you've been on the road too long without a stop. The town is immaculately clean, coolly tree-lined. Despite the golden light and Spanish adobe of California, its leisurely, discreet atmosphere definitely smacks of New England. Southeast of the town is the **Carmel Mission,** Basilica San Carlos Borromeo del Río Carmelo. Its peacefulness perfectly complements the tranquillity of the town. Father Serra is buried there.

The **coast road** from Carmel to Big Sur is only 30 miles long, but it takes more than an hour of careful driving. The land- and seascapes are astonishing—inland the Santa Lucia mountains and the redwoods and sycamore of Los Padres National Forest, oceanside the sheer cliffs, rocky crags and a sparkling, rolling surf. Luckily there are plenty of stopping places.

Point Lobos State Reserve takes you right down to the sea where you can explore pools among the rocks at low tide for starfish, hermit crabs and sea urchins. Resist the temptation to take the delicious urchins because this is a state-protected reserve that insists you look but don't touch. The cormorants and sea-gulls up on the rocks of Bird Island ignore the laws and help themselves. Look out for colonies of sea-otters, most strictly protected by this game refuge (their skins were much prized by traders in the past), and, in November, the grey whales heading south for the winter.

Big Sur and the Pfeiffer-Big Sur State Park offer marvellous opportunities for picnics, camping, hiking and fishing in the Big Sur River. This was the home of writer Henry Miller. Other artists still live there and you'll find it a great place to escape the crowd. Back on the coast, Orson Welles built a redwood honeymoon cottage for Rita Hayworth in the days when film stars did the romantic things expected of them. Now it's been expanded into a restaurant, worth a visit for its matchless view of the ocean, if nothing else.

The rugged shoreline road continues down 65 more miles to where William Randolph Hearst, the man Orson Welles immortalized in Citizen Kane, built his unbelievable dream castle at **San Simeon**. (Allow at least two hours for the guided tours. It's advisable to make a reservation, especially in the summer crush, by phoning 1-800-444-PARK, from out of the state, or 619-452-1950, from within.)

When you first see the Hearst castle dominating a ridge in front of the Santa Lucia mountains facing the Pacific, you might not accept it as real. You'd be right.

The thing is total fantasy. Nothing real could look like a Spanish cathedral, a Roman palace and a Gothic castle at the same time. So what is it? Hearst himself solved the problem by referring to the 123 acres of castle, guest-house palazzos, terraces, gardens, Roman baths, private zoo and tennis courts as "the Ranch". The central building, with its twin 137-foot towers modelled after the single-towered Ronda Cathedral in Spain was called "the Ranch Hotel". Hearst built it all with money acquired from his father's copper-mining fortune and his own publishing empire of 26 newspapers, 9 magazines and sundry news and photo agencies that saw its heyday in the 1920s. Building began in 1919 and was not completed by Hearst's death in 1951.

It's 1,600 feet up in the hills, 5 miles from the sea, commanding an estate of 275,000 acres (farmed for cattle by the Hearst family while the "Hearst San Simeon Historical Monument" is administered by the State of California). In your tour-bus—you park your car at the foot of the hill—you'll pass zebras, barbary sheep and goats grazing on the slopes, remnants of Hearst's zoo that once included a polar bear, lions, cheetahs, a leopard, panther and monkeys. His guests included Winston Churchill, **49**

Charlie Chaplin, Zelda and Scott Fitzgerald, Greta Garbo and George Bernard Shaw.

San Francisco architect Julia Morgan built the "Ranch" to Hearst's specifications as a "functional showcase" for his art collection. The mind-boggling mixture of that collection begins

No Greeks or Romans in the pool at Hearst's Castle in San Simeon.

to register as you pass the 104-foot swimming pool with its Greek colonnade and a copy of Donatello's Florentine statue of David standing on two original 17th-century Baroque Venetian fountains that Hearst joined together. A Roman sarcophagus and 3,500-year-old Egyptian goddess are both authentic, but the "Ranch House" façade, its equestrian friezes on the balcony and Gothic canopies are made of

reinforced concrete. Built, Hearst insisted, to withstand any earthquake that might open up the nearby San Andreas fault. Over the gigantic main entrance, in quiet simplicity, is a genuine 13th-century Madonna and Child.

Inside, the hodge-podge runs riot. A vestibule with a 60 B.C. Roman mosaic floor takes you to a salon with 15th-century Flemish tapestries over Italian choir stalls behind sofas that have 1930s slip-covers borrowing motifs from the tapestries. The dining room has a magnificent cedarwood coffer ceiling from a Bologna monastery and is decorated with the flags from the Sienna *palio* pageant. At the table set for 22 guests, Hearst's sense of proportion was emphasized by his splendid Queen Anne silver candlesticks and wine-cisterns set beside tomato ketchup, pickles and mustard served in their original bottles and jars.

After this improbable castle you may want to retreat into the world of the 18th century with a visit to the **La Purisima Mission** at LOMPOC (freeway 101 south to Santa Maria, then route 1 to Lompoc). Founded in 1787 and rebuilt in 1813 after an earthquake, the restored pink and white adobe mission offers a haven of peace amid the old living and working quarters of the missionaries, soldiers and Indians. Still there are the tallow-vats used for making soap and candles, looms on which the Indians were taught weaving, a screw-press for olive oil, gristmill for flour and the old wine-barrels in a cellar. The soldiers' quarters show their weapons and camp-beds. In the chapel you'll see a 1799 carved wooden sacristy chest and the priests' origi-

nal vestments. The garden is full of olive and mulberry trees. There's an adobe hut in the Indian village set aside for unmarried girls, keeping them, as the missionaries stipulated, "secure from every insult"—a Spanish but not necessarily Indian custom. (The mission grounds today include a garden for visitors' picnics.)

Los Angeles

Los Angeles is the quintessential 20th-century creation. Only modern technology could have turned this desert into one of the most flourishing metropolises on earth. Engineering genius brought water hundreds of miles across mountains and deserts to feed the city and its industry and nurture its eucalyptus and palm trees and lush gardens. The people scattered across its vast area and the car with its fabled freeway system arrived in time to link them up in one burgeoning monster that never ceases to astonish.

People who don't know it complain that Los Angeles is nothing but a bunch of suburbs looking for a city. The cliché is not so much untrue as irrelevant. When you visit the various neighbourhoods and townships that make up greater Los Angeles—Hollywood, Westwood, Santa Monica, Malibu, and dozens more—you find that nobody's looking for a city, they know where they are. Up in the hills, down at the beach, in the valley, around the university campus, they're all integral parts of Los Angeles. It is not a city in the traditional sense of a downtown urban core interacting with surrounding neighbourhoods, outskirts and suburbs, L.A. is more a state of mind. And a huge state of mind at that, covering 460 square miles bounded by sea and sand to the west, by mountains to the north and east and by desert to the south, with an almost permanent canopy of sun to top it off. With all these possibilities, it's not surprising that leisure and pleasure are worshipped here.

"The Beach"
The beach (Angelenos always refer to it in the singular, one whole concept) stretches some 40 miles from Malibu through Santa Monica, Venice, Marina del Rey, Hermosa and Redondo to Palos Verdes before the white sands hit the pollution of Los Angeles Harbour and the Long

To appreciate L.A., you must love the beach—and the freeway system.

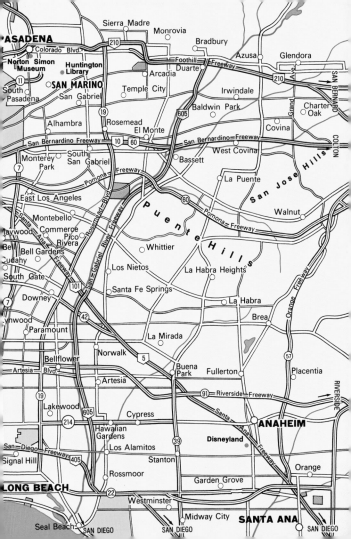

Beach shipyards. And there's no better way to get the special feel of Los Angeles than going straight down there. In L.A., beaches are not just resorts for holidays and week-end cottages, they are year-round residential areas.

Malibu is the favoured beach home of the more relaxed members of the film community. Rather than barricade themselves behind electrified fences guarded by Doberman pinschers as they do in Bel Air and Beverly Hills, film stars and hot young directors can be seen jogging along the sands or shopping for yoghurt and diet drinks in the supermarket. Malibu Lagoon's Surf-rider Beach attracts champion surfers from all over the world. Sunning and swimming are a little more peaceful down at Las Tunas and Topanga. Malibu Pier is a good place to fish. The one hazard disturbing Malibu's sunny peace is the occasional "cat's paw" tide or mountain landslide that wash-es the handsome beach-houses into the Pacific.

Santa Monica is built on more solid ground, befitting the solid middle class town it is, and its beaches are more of a family affair. But it's neighbouring **Venice** that attracts all the attention. The beach and beach-park here are a non-stop open-air amateur circus of freaks, acrobats, weightlifters, clowns and jugglers entertaining themselves quite as much as the passing crowd. In 1892, millionaire Albert Kinney had wanted to set down on the Pacific coast a replica of Italy's Venice, complete with canals, gondolas, a palazzo or two, hotels and amusement arcades. Then somebody discovered oil and the idea was abandoned. Four canals remain with a Lighthouse Bridge that traverses the lagoon area feeding the canals. The neighbourhood has revived as a diverse community of serious artists, upscale galleries and the ever-present

Cops on Wheels

Every craze gets a try-out in Venice. Roller-skaters boogie their way along specially marked paths to music from dozens of radios set around the grass and all tuned to the same station. The fresh sea breezes mingle with the perfume of coconut suntan oil and the smoke of strange weeds. Los Angeles Police Department officers watch over it all more or less benignly, also equipped with roller skates and dressed in black running shorts and white T-shirts with "L.A.P.D." on the chest. For those that don't spot the initials, the guns in the holsters make it clear who's the law around here.

56

Film stars will stoop to con- quer—even in cement if neces- sary. But be sure to spell their names right.

bohemian types. Venice artists pioneered the street-painting that has spread through the Los Angeles area—hyper-realist murals covering whole façades often three and four storeys high, some creating optical illusions by depicting perfect mirror images of the street on which they appear. In this region of instant obsolescence, the murals come and go, but Venice seems to have an on-going collection.

Movieland

London buries its heroes in Westminster Abbey, Paris puts great Frenchmen to rest in the Pantheon, and Los Angeles offers the hand, foot and hoof prints of its stars in the cement courtyard of **Mann's Chinese Theatre** (at 6925 Hollywood Boulevard). Start your pilgrim- age here. Sid Grauman had the idea in 1927 of getting the immortals' prints when they attended gala premieres at his great exotic cinema. Most stars did the same as Mary Pickford, the Marx Brothers and Rita Hayworth: got down on their knees and made a hand print, but it was natural for Fred Astaire to leave a foot print and cowboy Tom Mix preferred leaving the hoof print of his horse. If you go to see a film in L.A.—and it would seem silly not to, like not eating in Paris—go to one of the old preposterous movie palaces like the Chinese or the Egyptian across the street. The outrageous pagoda and Theban temple décors may be better than the film.

Walk along **Hollywood Boulevard**—one of the parts of L.A. where walking is customary—and you'll see over 2,500 actors' names on bronze stars imbedded in the pavement. The street itself is less scintillating—rundown shops and pizza parlours, but the second-hand bookstores are excellent. You'll pass Frederic's of Hollywood with its lingerie museum and the beautifully restored Roosevelt Hotel. Between La Brea and Western Avenue, the boulevard has the fine tacky splendour of the 1920s and 30s, with its low flat stucco buildings and a droopy palm tree or two; even some vintage pre-war Packards and Buicks parked on the street.

A few blocks north of the boulevard is **Hollywood Bowl,** the splendid open-air auditorium where the Los Angeles Philharmonic Orchestra holds concerts against a background of the gigantic illuminated letters of H-O-L-L-Y-W-O-O-D planted up in the hills.

South of Hollywood Boulevard is L.A.'s most famous street, **Sunset Boulevard.** The Hollywood section of it is known simply as "The Strip". It's where people cruise up and down in convertibles looking at each other, on a street of sleazy nightclubs and cheap motels side by side with hip boutiques and elegant restaurants. Pretty young ladies and gentlemen stand there waiting at night.

An important part of the landscape here are the extravagant billboards advertising the latest releases of the record companies. For Hollywood's claim to being the entertainment capital of America stems not only from its film and television studios but also from its recording studios for popular music, symbolized by the Capitol Tower shaped like a stack of records on Vine Street.

Further west, the boulevard turns residential with the great mansions of the moguls. While these homes are heavily guarded, you can sense the opulent atmosphere by stopping for a drink at the plush Beverly Hills Hotel, where visiting stars, directors and writers sign their contracts (not autographs) in the Polo Lounge.

Since this is a pilgrimage, you may want to visit a few shrines—the homes of the stars in Beverly Hills. Bus companies used to take the worshipful into the posh suburb and point them out until coaches were banned. But the really determined will find their own way using an "Official Map to the Stars' Homes".

Beverly Hills is exclusive and assertively separate from Los Angeles. The streets are lined with Rolls Royces and Mercedes and the architecture of the mansions is an astounding mixture of Spanish, Gothic, Bauhaus and Renaissance, in every pastel shade imaginable.

The town is phenomenally clean and litter is almost a capital crime. It's policed with formidable efficiency and, except for the great shopping streets such as Rodeo Drive (see p. 93), walking is viewed with suspicion, especially at night. If you do want to take a walk here, put on tennis or jogging clothes and the police will assume you're a sportsman. Only burglars, it seems, walk around Beverly Hills in normal clothes.

One of the most enjoyable Hollywood trips is a **tour of the film and television studios.** Two major TV networks (CBS and NBC) welcome you onto the sets for a look behind the scenes at some of America's most popular shows. A limited number of tickets to live shows are available on request. Universal Studios (Lankershim Boulevard, north of the Hollywood Freeway) offers an elaborate tour in open trolleys with guides who have all the show-biz flair of Hollywood itself. Participating in the special effects trickery, you'll be attacked by space-ships and the shark from *Jaws,* you'll meet up with a 3-storey-tall King Kong and generally be subjected to all the earthquakes, flash floods and fires you ever saw in a disaster film. You'll visit sound stages and back-lots, and learn the screen techniques used to create film's great illusions. You'll see how Moses parted the waters of the Red Sea in *The Ten Commandments* and ride through a town that offers a New England fishing-village, a Bavarian square, French bistros and an Italian pizzeria all in the space of four blocks.

Warner Brothers and Columbia are both housed at Burbank Studios (Hollywood Way, off the Ventura Freeway) and they organize a tour for smaller groups through special effects and prop departments and around back-lots, sometimes, if you're lucky, even during shooting.

While you're up on the north side of town, take a ride around the Hollywood Hills for a superb

view of Los Angeles. Watch the smog come and go or just sit there and dream. On a clear day you can see Long Beach. Up here, tucked away in Laurel Canyon or Nichols Canyon, more of the film community hide out, especially writers, who like the seclusion. Most of the houses, with obligatory swimming pools, are handsomely designed and perch precariously on the

The studios give you a chance to play a couple of 1930s gangsters or to be scared by a rubber shark.

edge of the mountain, right over a gaping chasm.

There's a more scholarly side to Los Angeles, around the **campus of UCLA** (University of California—Los Angeles) at Westwood Village; more scholarly but still a lot of fun. Westwood is a great place to stroll around, go to the best cinemas in town, enjoy the café life, eat an ice-cream, buy a pair of tennis shoes, a frisbee or even a book. If Hollywood has filled you with a new gratitude for the joys of cinema, you might like to pay homage to Marilyn Monroe in Westwood Memorial Park (1212 Glendon Avenue, south of Wilshire Boulevard), where a modest plaque bears silent testimony to the actress.

Downtown

Downtown Los Angeles is steadily becoming a more attractive and culturally active community. Some of the downtown institutions that have surfaced in recent years include the Museum of Contemporary Art (see p. 63) and the Los Angeles Contemporary Exhibitions. The **Music Center** (at First Street and Grand) is important for concerts and plays at the Dorothy Chandler Pavilion, the Mark Taper Forum and Ahmanson Theater. The colourful Mexican (Chicano) life of the city is best enjoyed at **Grand Central Market,** north of Pershing Square. (The other great food market is Farmer's Market, at Fairfax and Third.)

Watts, besides being famous as the black neighbourhood of Los Angeles that erupted in violent anger in 1965, offers one of the city's more bizarre and somehow exhilarating monuments, the **Watts Towers** (1765 East 107th Street, off the Harbor Freeway). In 1921 a tile-setter named Simon Rodia started to erect three tapering towers of coloured pottery shards, sea shells, glass and pebbles cemented to frames of scrap steel and baling wire. When he'd raised the towers 104 feet, 33 years later, he announced that he'd achieved his ambition "to do something big" and walked away, never to be heard of again. The towers are in the great tradition of L.A. as a home of fantasy needing no rational explanation.

If you're going west again from downtown, avoid the freeway and take another great thoroughfare, **Wilshire Boulevard,** shining with the prosperity of its department stores and big hotels, but also a living museum of the ornate art deco architecture that characterized L.A.'s rise to greatness in the 1920s and 30s. You'll see other examples around town, especially in **61**

Hollywood, but Wilshire is a good place to look out for them: **I. Magnin's** at the corner of Kingsley, the Franklin Life insurance building at Van Ness, and the 5209 Wilshire, among others. Several miles west, near the entrance to Westwood Village, are several more architectural jewels, designed by such world-renowned architects as Helmut Jahn, Romaldo Giurgola and Larrabee Barnes. At the

Design in L.A. has its own modern style; from I. M. Pei's Century City towers to Neo-Americano Popcorn.

south-west corner of Beverly Hills, Century City is becoming a mini-downtown, with some of the best-looking skyscrapers, including I.M. Pei's twin three-sided towers.

HOT POPCORN FRESH

Museums

Traditionally, L.A. has resisted the idea of museums. But that's all changing as two rival institutions pull in the crowds: the revamped **L.A. County Museum** (5905 Wilshire Boulevard) with its burgeoning 20th-century art collection and striking Pavilion for Japanese Art, and the **Museum of Contemporary Art** (MOCA) at California Plaza. MOCA curators keep ahead of the pack by commissioning new work, on display alongside the contemporary classics. A satellite of MOCA, the **Temporary Contemporary** in Central Avenue is a popular (and permanent) museum of post-war art.

Also worthy of note are private collections such as the **Norton Simon Museum** at Pasadena (Orange Grove and Colorado, off the Ventura Freeway). In a handsome modern

63

structure Norton Simon put together in only two decades of collecting a truly remarkable range of European paintings, drawings and sculpture from the early Renaissance to the 20th century, along with Indian bronzes and Asian stone carvings. The outstanding Italian works include two superb Madonnas by Raphael and Botticelli, admirable early works by Filippino Lippi and Lorenzetti;

18th-century Venice is also well represented by Tiepolo and Canaletto. Rubens' *Holy Women at the Sepulchre* is one of his true masterpieces, as are Rembrandt's *Self-Portrait* and *Titus*.

Among the delights of the Norton Simon Collection in Pasadena are the sculptured bronzes of Degas.

Spain offers one of the jewels of the collection in Zurbarán's lovely *Still-Life with Lemons, Orange and a Rose*, as well as Goya's fine *Saint Jerome*. French painting is richly endowed here—Poussin, Watteau, Manet's magnificent *Ragpicker*, Cézanne's *Chestnut Trees and Farm*. There's an extensive collection of Picasso drawings and one of the museum's great joys are the Degas bronzes. The sculpture garden includes works by Maillol, Picasso, Rodin, Giacometti and Henry Moore.

While you're in Pasadena, drive down to the **Huntington Library** (1151 Oxford in neighbouring San Marino). Its staggering collection of books includes one of the few surviving First Folios of William Shakespeare, a Gutenberg Bible and Benjamin Franklin's manuscript of his autobiography. In the art gallery you'll find the original painting of the English-speaking world's most popular jigsaw puzzle, Thomas Gainsborough's *Blue Boy*, part of an outstanding assembly of British painting. But perhaps the Huntington's most seductive attraction is the **Botanical Garden.** Choose among the Japanese garden, the palm garden, the desert garden and the Shakespeare garden, where Huntington planted almost every shrub and flower mentioned by the Great Bard in that First Folio up at the house.

The **J. Paul Getty Museum** (17985 W. Pacific Coast Highway, Malibu—call ahead 458-2003 for reserved parking in the museum garage) is somewhere between the Norton Simon collection and Hearst Castle. It's undoubtedly a serious art collection, but its setting in a vast replica of a palatial Roman villa shares something of the ambitious inclinations of San Simeon, though without the flamboyance—or the humour. But Getty had a more coherent idea of what he liked—Greek and Roman, Renaissance, Baroque and French Rococo, and that was it. On a visit to the archaeological sites of Pompeii and Herculaneum, Getty fell in love with the Villa dei Papiri, excavated in the 18th century from volcanic mud left by the eruption of Mount Vesuvius in A.D. 79. From the Herculaneum ruin, he found it was possible to reconstruct—more or less—what it had looked like. The Malibu museum is the result. The reconstruction is a painstaking replica of the luxurious villa, complete with mosaics, geometric gardens and Corinthian colonnades (of plastered concrete), using marble and terrazzo for the floors and paving. It cost $17 million to build and, dying before it was **65** opened in 1974, Getty left most of his huge oil fortune to the museum for future acquisitions. The collection of antiquities is impressive, highlighted by **"the Getty bronze"**, a 4th-century B.C. statue of an Olympic champion, believed by some experts to be the only existing work of Lysippus, court sculptor of Alexander the Great. The paintings include works by Raphael, Rubens, Van Dyck and Rembrandt.

Los Angeles South

Orange County is bedrock Southern California, land of the fabled little old ladies in tennis shoes; but for visitors its most remarkable feature is **Anaheim.** If Hollywood is Los Angeles' dream-factory, where the dreams are manufactured for distribution worldwide, then Anaheim is a dream-supermarket, where you can drive up and buy your dream right there for instant consumption.

Anaheim (27 miles southeast of downtown L.A. on the Santa Ana freeway) is the home of **Disneyland.** Since 1955, Walt Disney and his successors have been dispensing the good clean pleasures of a make-believe world inspired by the sweet uplifting fantasies of his films. Applying the techniques of the cinema and advanced electronics technology, Disney takes you around his smiling Techni-coloured "theme park" on a day-long outing that is simply stupefying in scope and impact. You buy a 1-, 2- or 3-day Passport covering the whole Disneyland complex, good for unlimited use of the attractions.

"Main Street" sets the tone with its sunny evocation of small-town U.S.A. at the turn of the century. You may notice that the houses and shops are all three-quarter size. In this effort to escape from the realities of the outside world, everything's a little smaller than life. "Adventureland" is a boat ride through simulated jungle foliage on a river that passes successively through Asia, Africa and the South Pacific, complete with plastic tigers and alligators, stuffed elephants and hairy gorillas that emit tape-recorded roars and beat their chests. A miniature railroad takes you through "Frontierland", the pioneer country of the Old West where a loudspeaker warns you to "watch out for Indians and wild animals". Just the faintest uneasiness is aroused by a settler's cabin on fire with a wax-model pioneer lying outside, killed by an Indian's arrow. But at the end of each ride are ice-cream and soft-drinks stands. One of the most exciting themes is "Tomor-

rowland", constantly being reno-
vated to keep pace with progress.
The rides include a submarine, a
spaceship to Mars and up-to-date
experiments in public transport.

North-west of Disneyland is
the **Movieland Wax Museum**
(7711 Beach Boulevard, Buena

*Adults like to pretend they go to
Disneyland for their kids' sake.*

Park) which sets out its wax
figures of film stars in scenes
from their best-known films.
Understandably, the most life- **67**

like are those stars who were the most impassive on screen: Gary Cooper, Alan Ladd, Yul Brynner. The Marx Brothers are less successful. Gene Kelly, in *Singing In the Rain,* is unconvincing because he's not dancing and it's not raining. Poor Brigitte Bardot is presented with a certain sexy pneumatic likeness but the sign beside her reads: "as she was XX years ago" with the number of years interchangeable like the number of billions of McDonald's hamburgers eaten around the world.

The most interesting display in the museum for film buffs is the collection of old nickelodeons, autoscopes and movieola machines that showed the very first moving pictures—still on show—with titles like "Tessie the Tease", "Before the Bath" and "After the Bath" (but not "During the Bath").

The museum has an annexe that is perhaps the most astounding exhibition in all of California: the **Palace of Living Art.** It's a collection of some of the world's great art masterpieces presented as three-dimensional wax-effigy tableaux. Leonardo da Vinci is honoured with two works—*The Last Supper* and the *Mona Lisa,* whose enigmatic smile has become positively bewildering. El Greco's *Cardinal de Guevara* looks startled at what's happened to him. But Toulouse-Lautrec is accorded the greatest distinction. He is included as an effigy with all his famous Montmartre figures posing for one composite tableau. Seeing is believing.

South of the Wax Museum, **Knott's Berry Farm** produces a different kind of fantasy, bringing to life America's wild west in three different theme park areas. Rides, attractions, shops and a

Long Beach is proud of its naval tradition and a spectacular coast.

"Good Time Theatre" will keep you entertained for hours.

Long Beach—actually the beach is 7 miles long—is worth a visit if you like looking at boats. It has one of the world's biggest, the **Queen Mary,** permanently moored here as a nostalgic reminder of "the good old days". Its staterooms have been converted into a hotel, its dining rooms into a restaurant and the rest is open for tours. Here, too, is Howard Hughes's phenomenal **Spruce Goose.** Developed as a troop carrier during World War II, the "flying boat" clocked one mile on its maiden voyage—and never flew again.

San Diego

This is where California's history began, where Juan Rodríguez Cabrillo, a Portuguese captain, first set foot on Californian soil in 1542. Sixty years later, its bay was explored for Spanish galleons to stop off at on their way to and from the South Pacific, but it wasn't until 1769 that Father Serra built his first mission. Today, San Diego is California's second largest city.

The best way to appreciate San Diego's sparkling beauty is from the sea. Take a **cruise** along the Bay—they start from Harbor

Drive at the end of Broadway— past the man-made Harbor and Shelter Islands around the tip of the peninsula to Point Loma out on the Pacific. The fishing, sailing and U.S. Navy vessels make for a splendidly varied skyline.

Back on dry land, you can visit one of the 19th-century ships moored on the Embarcadero as part of the Maritime Museum Fleet, the most picturesque being the iron-hulled *Star of India* built in 1863. Or drop into Seaport Village, a lively complex of shops, restaurants and galleries.

San Diego's discoverer is celebrated by the **Cabrillo National Monument** on the Point Loma promontory (follow the signs south-west on Rosecrans Street). Cabrillo's statue, donated by the Portuguese government, faces the spot at which he landed.

Old Town (bounded by Juan, Twiggs, Congress and Wallace Streets) is a six-block area of restored adobe buildings from the city's Mexican era. You'll enjoy a rest under the palms and eucalyptus of Plaza Vieja, originally the centre and bullfight arena before the Yankees arrived.

The modern town is blessed with enlightened urban planning, the popular Horton Plaza shopping-center—and the superb **Balboa Park.** Set right in the centre of town, the park has a wealth of sports facilities—tennis, golf, baseball, badminton and lawn bowling—as well as museums around El Prado (the Promenade), including a Fine Arts Gallery, space and anthropological museums.

But the highlight of the park is devoted to the animals in the **San Diego Zoo,** justly acclaimed as one of the world's finest. Certainly the 128-acre zoo is one of the most humane, giving the animals as large, free and natural a living space as is possible in the confines of a man-made park. Zoologists have provided canyons, grottos and a tropical rain-forest. The collection of animals is particularly strong in Australian species—kangaroo, wallaby, koala and a wonderful assortment of exotic birds. You can fly over the whole zoo in the Skyfari aerial tramway or take a guided tour-bus. You're also allowed to walk.*

Another great park is at **Mission Bay,** offering first class aquatic facilities. Paddle around tiny islands and lagoons in canoes or sail in catamarans and full-size sloops. It is also the

This San Diego archway reflects the city's old Spanish tradition.

---

*An extension of the zoo, the San Diego Wild Animal Park—north on Interstate highway 15 and east at the Via Rancho exit—offers 1,800 acres more for elephants and other species that need the space to roam in a landscape reminiscent of East African savanna.

71

home of **Sea World,** where you will see the famous three-ton killer whale and its baby, not to mention the trained seal lions, otters and a walrus who perform in the "Pirates of Pinnipeds". Something for everyone in this aquatic entertainment mixing scares and laughs.

The beaches here are truly beautiful and remarkably unspoiled, stretching 27 miles up to elegant **La Jolla** (pronounced La Hoya). The latter's Windansea and Boomer beaches are marvellous for surfing. It's a popular resort for artists and the La Jolla Museum of Contemporary Arts is well worth a look.

National Parks

If the great outdoors is a religion in California, then the National Parks of Yosemite, Sequoia/ Kings Canyon and the National Monument of Death Valley are its temples. They are magnificent stretches of wilderness in which to recapture the adventurous spirit of the earliest American experience—in the Sierra Nevada mountains, the huge silent forests and the awe-inspiring desert. They are of course popular with tourists, Yosemite much more so than the others, but they are all large enough for you to hike, ride, ski or climb away from the rest of the world. You may find yourself tramping up a trail with half a dozen other groups, but only walk a hundred yards further and you'll be alone again; the mountains, trees, rocks are all yours.

The National Parks are protected by the Federal Government and certain regulations must be observed. There are strict speed limits on the park roads, for the most part lower than on normal highways. It is forbidden to feed or otherwise interfere with the wild animals you may encounter. Hunting is illegal and fishing requires a state licence. Certain areas are closed to camping and fires are severely restricted to designated areas (heavy fines are charged to those discovered by rangers), but none of these regulations is a real burden as there are excellent public barbecue and accommodation facilities.

Each of the parks is four or five hours' drive from the coast, but well worth the effort. The best times of year for Yosemite and Sequoia are spring and autumn, but there isn't a bad time of year. Winter offers some good cross-country and even downhill skiing in Yosemite and lovely snow-scapes in Sequoia, but you should check ahead to find out which roads are closed.

Summer in both parks is high season and relatively crowded, but the peace of the high country is always within reach. Death Valley is best from late autumn through winter to early spring, but even summer, with the proper preparations and precautions for the heat, is a memorable experience.

Yosemite

"Base camp", which may be a plush hotel room, more modest lodge accommodation or simply a tent, is at the heart of Yosemite Valley along the Merced River. From the valley meadow, you can hike, bike (rentals at Yosemite Lodge or Curry Village) or take the shuttle bus to all the great sights. Soaring granite domes enclose the valley—Half Dome at the north-east end (8,842 feet above sea-level), Glacier Point, Sentinel and Cathedral Spires down the south wall and El Capitan, Three Brothers and Washington Column up the north wall.

You can grade the hikes according to your capacity and endurance, but try at least one hike, in sturdy shoes, for the sheer exhilaration of making it to the end. In the Merced River Canyon, **Vernal Falls** is within the scope of any normally healthy person, along a well-marked path that begins at Happy Isles Nature Center, where knowledgeable U.S. Rangers will answer your questions. The brilliant light and intoxicatingly clean air on the trail through the pine trees are a delight.

If you're up to it, push on along the Mist Trail, past Emerald Pool to **Nevada Falls** and you'll begin to lose the crowd. Here you're on the John Muir Trail, named after the Scottish naturalist who explored the Sierra Nevada and made their conservation against the encroachments of civilization his life's work. The trail goes on past Merced Lake and heads for the lovely **Tuolumne Meadows** in the high country; final destination: Mount Whitney, that's more than 200 miles away—Muir did it, but it's perhaps a little more than you want to do on this trip.

Less exhausting is a drive or shuttle-bus ride past Badger Pass (good skiing slopes in winter) to **Glacier Point.** It's 7,214 feet above sea level. Both the altitude and the view over the whole valley and the High Sierras beyond are, yes, breathtaking. You can see Yosemite Creek drop half a mile from the opposite wall in two spectacular plunges—Upper and Lower **Yosemite Falls**—and you'll get an outstanding view of 73

the majestic Half Dome. From here you may be willing to leave the bus and hike and picnic on your way back, along the Panorama Trail via the Nevada and Vernal Falls, 8 miles in all, downhill.

One other beautiful hike is out to **Mirror Lake,** especially in spring or early summer when the waters are perfectly still in the early morning or at sunset, capturing the most marvellous colours from the trees and Mount Watkins behind it.

Sequoia/Kings Canyon National Park

You'll doubtless be needing a moment of peace among the giant sequoias, many of them approaching 3,000 years old. The forest offers a gorgeous array of dogwoods, sugar pines and white firs as well, and a rich flora of orange leopard lily, white corn lily, lupine, chinquapin and bracken fern. You may start out a city slicker but a few hours in Sequoia will make you a nature-lover for life. This is no place for a hurried look; bide your time,

For peace of mind there's nothing to match Yosemite's back country.

walk slowly, sit quietly and listen, fall asleep under a tree. Watch for the birds—woodpecker, raven, spotted owl, but also W.C. Field's favourite, the mountain chickadee, and a cheeky fellow known as the Steller's Jay.

Start at the Giant Forest Village with its motel, and the Park Ranger's Visitors Center at Lodgepole. Get a map and information about the best walks in the forest and hikes in the back country. They show a good documentary film about the sequoias.

The best introduction to the forest is **Congress Trail.** It's an easy two-mile mile walk, but worth lingering over for a couple of hours to absorb the beauty of the largest living creations in nature. The trail begins at the **General Sherman Tree,** biggest of all, 275 feet high, 103 feet around its base and still growing. Reaching up for their light well above the rest of the forest, the branches start 130 feet above the ground. As you move among the other great sequoias—the President, the Senate Group, the House Group and the General Lee, you can understand old John Muir waxing lyrical about "the first tree in the forest to feel the touch of rosy beams of morning and the last to bid the sun goodnight." It's worth getting up at dawn and coming back again at sunset to see the sequoias enjoy that special privilege.

Another beautiful walk, by no means an exhausting hike, is out to **Crescent Meadow,** passing such venerable trees as the Bear's Bathtub, the Shattered Giant and the Chimney.

If you want to get away and explore the back country, carry on along the High Sierra Trail for the 11 miles from Crescent Meadow to **Bearpaw Meadow.** This is a not too formidable hike and has a rudimentary back-country camp to rest in. A nearby lake and streams offer good fishing, especially for trout. You'll have a fair chance of spotting some of the park's wild-life—bobcats, coyotes, golden eagles, black bear, spotted skunk and cougar.

Death Valley National Monument

A convenient way to see Death Valley is to combine it with an excursion to Las Vegas (see p. 80) and come in from the east, either on highway 95 and via Death Valley Junction on 190, or further north via Beatty, on 58. (The southern route from L.A., via Mojave and Trona, is long and tiresome.)

This desert is perhaps the great surprise of all the wonders of California. It's not one but a dozen landscapes, not a monot-onous expanse of sand dunes but an endless variety of terrains, rock-formations, colours and plants. Go there in winter and you may see a flood of spring flowers blooming in the wake of the sparse rains that the Panamint Mountains deign to let into the

---

Good and Bad Fires

On your travels around the park, you'll come across the scars of past fires on some of the sequoia trees. These are the result of wildfires (accidental or nature-caused, such as by lightning), prescribed fires (purposely started by park rangers), or pre-scribed natural fires (started by natural causes and allowed to burn out on their own). You may even encounter a prescribed fire in action. They will be well marked by signs telling you "do not panic, do not report, do not extinguish".

Sequoias in fact need fires to survive. The fires sterilize harmful parasite insects and fungus in the soil and burn away excessive undergrowth that prevents new trees from sprouting. The sequoia has a thick bark that insulates the growing por-tion of the tree from fire damage. The bark, fluted like a Greek column, can mea-sure more than two feet thick and you'll see many trees with a concave hollow caused by historic fires. They still flourish hundreds, maybe thousands of years later. The rangers' fires are just supportive therapy.

valley from the west. But above all, there's the light, uncannily clear, distorting distances, pink at dawn, white at mid-morning, piercing silver at noon and then shimmering into gold as the afternoon progresses.

Don't be put off by the name, Death Valley. It was bequeathed from the bitter hardships of the gold-rush hopefuls who crossed from Arizona and Nevada. Some never made it, but they didn't have air-conditioned cars or the excellent resort facilities at the oasis of FURNACE CREEK. A motel or luxury inn offers first-class accommodation or, if you're roughing it, you can use the camp-grounds.

Get up at dawn—really, you won't regret it—and drive out south-east along highway 190 to **Zabriskie Point.** As the sun rises behind you, the light hits Tucki Mountain and the tips of the Panamints to the west before plunging into the valley's pri-meval salt lake-bed below. This parched and deserted no-man's land is likely to set you wonder-ing about the world's creation. By mid-morning (if you visit in winter) the temperature will still be in the cool 50s on your ex-posed ridge, but walk down the hill to the lake-bed and you'll feel the heat rising to meet you, reaching the 80s by the time you get to the bottom.

Continue over to **Dante's View** (altitude 5,745 feet) look-ing down at Badwater, 282 feet below sea-level. It is the lowest point in the United States. Make up your own mind whether this is paradise, purgatory or hell. On the other side of the valley you can see, from north to south, Wildrose, Bennett and Telescope Peaks.

Retrace the road back again towards Furnace Creek and turn off left, travelling along the Death Valley floor. Follow the crumbling lake-bed known as the Devil's Golf Course as far as **Badwater** and walk out across that expanse of baked salt. The degree of desolation is almost exhilarating. Look closer at the salt and you'll discover it's set into bizarre funnel shapes, swirls and other intricate patterns. Drive back north again and cut off at the arrow pointing to **Artist's Drive.** Here you can explore a canyon of multi-coloured rocks and shrubs that culminates in the aptly-named **Artist's Palette.** The rocks have oxidized into bright mauve, ver-milion, ochre, lime green, tur-quoise and purple.

Death Valley was an irre-sistible magnet for optimistic miners—copper, lead, gold, sil-ver and borax. But only the latter paid off, most of the others prov-ing duds. One gold mine hit paydirt, $3 million in two years, and when you drive out west from the valley, you can visit the ghost-town the miners left behind, **Skidoo,** along the road down Emigrant Canyon.

At the end of your drive, at the northern boundary of Death Valley, you can visit **Scotty's Castle.** This luxuriously furnished mansion in its unlikely setting was constructed in the early 1900s by an eccentric millionaire in search of solitude. The castle takes its name from its caretaker, Scotty.

Excursion to Las Vegas

If, as we claim, European dreamers go to America and American dreamers go to California, where do California dreamers go? Well, they take Interstate Highway 15 from Los Angeles north-east across the Mojave Desert and over the Nevada state line to Las Vegas. Whilst the resort may have been considered Sodom and Gomorrah with air-conditioning and neon lights, today it seeks to

project a wholesome image as an internationally known city hosting massive conventions and major sporting events, and welcoming millions of tourists. The city has a resident population of 800,000—for the most part living in fancy retirement complexes on the outskirts of town—that enjoys a wealth of cultural and sports amenities offered by the area's health clubs, art centres and numerous churches.

Squeaky-clean aura notwithstanding, Las Vegas remains one of those myth-laden towns that everybody should see before they die. No amount of familiarity with films showing the marvels of this gambler's paradise can quite prepare you for the shock of the real thing.

At **Casino Center** downtown, which has banks and professional buildings cheek to jowl with casinos, the neon lights are so overpoweringly bright that midnight can look like noon back in the Mojave. Focus for the action is up-and-coming **Fremont,** better known as "Glitter Gulch". Every lit-up window shows dozens of people frenetically tugging the levers of the "one-armed bandit" slot-machines. A sign says: "For every U.S. coin you got, we got the slot." Other signs invite you to "Cash your paycheck here" or "Exchange any foreign currency". They'll take your money any way you want to give it to them.

Primed with this first taste of things to come, head out to **The Strip** (officially Las Vegas Boulevard) between Sahara and Tropicana Avenues, four solid miles of hotels and casinos, each with a nightclub advertising America's top comedians and singers and a score of girlie-shows, on ice, in water, even on an ordinary stage. And by way of family entertainment, there's

Wet'n Wild, a vast water-theme park right on The Strip. You'll see wedding chapels attached to little motels, where you can get married for around $50, "witnesses extra" and spend your honeymoon next door. If it doesn't work out, you can get an instant divorce further along The Strip, at a slightly higher, fee.

Visit the most extravagant hotels on The Strip. These are the true monuments of Las Vegas, palaces of the Orient, Ancient Rome, Persia and many other fabled places that exist only in the minds of hotel and casino operators. The most outrageous are **Caesars Palace,** with its fountains and colonnades, the **Tropicana** and its Island Paradise, and the **Mirage** with its expansive gardens boasting waterfalls, palm trees and erupting volcano.

Las Vegas' enormous electricity bills are paid for by the losers.

But the décor is overwhelmed by the gambling, hundreds of slot-machines spill out from the casinos into the lobbies, roulette tables, baccarat, blackjack and bingo. Poker is usually played in a roped-off area at amazingly sedate tables. The most enjoyable tables to watch are the dice or craps games, where the players get excited, yell, whoop and groan as their fortunes go up and down. You'll notice there are no clocks, no windows in the casino—the management doesn't like you to think about what time of day it is; action is available round-the-clock.

Las Vegas has invented its own definition of sartorial and architectural understatement.

Even if you don't gamble, the spectacle in the casino is fascinating and the floor-shows in the nightclubs are first-rate. The best way to handle Las Vegas and survive is to arrive at sunset—for that view of the first neon lights in the desert—stay up all night, sleep late, have a good breakfast and leave immediately.

To clear your head, take a trip to Death Valley National Monument (see p. 76) or drive out to Lake Mead and Hoover Dam on

82

the Nevada/Arizona border, 30 miles south-east of Las Vegas. You can enjoy almost every water sport—fishing, sailing, windsurfing, water-skiing, scuba-diving, swimming, and boating—in **Lake Mead,** a huge three-basin lake in the Black Mountains, backed up behind the **Hoover Dam.** The dam itself across the Colorado River is a spectacular engineering achievement, its huge pylons creating a surprisingly attractive sculptural effect across the landscape. Take a guided tour. Stop off at historic **Boulder City,** a pretty community of neat lawns, built originally to house Hoover Dam workers, it will reassure you that Nevada has normal towns, too.

First settled in the early 1800s by Spanish explorers, Las Vegas really got going in 1931, when the Nevada state legislature voted to establish legalized casino gambling. Today over 18 million people visit the town, most of them to try their luck. About $3 billion is spent annually on gaming—much of it on the city's 85,000 slot machines, equipped to take from 1¢ to $500.

If you fancy having a go but have never played before, several casinos offer free gambling instruction before they'll take your money. But, even in the kingdom of Mammon, there are limits: you must be over 21 to enter a casino, or purchase alcohol.

What to Do

Sports

All sports are available in California from jogging to mountain climbing, from downhill skiing to snorkelling. But we start with what must be California's favourite.

Water Sports

If you get no other exercise while on holiday here, it would be difficult to go without at least one day swimming at the beach. It's no accident that most of America's swimming champions come from Southern California. In the middle-class neighbourhoods, every other house seems to have a swimming pool—from the air you can see a mass of turquoise blobs as you fly in to Los Angeles airport.

Surfing, snorkelling, scuba diving, wind surfing and water-skiing, sailing and fishing are all enjoyed along the coast. Everyone has his favourite beach or bay and some are better for one sport than another. Below we give an arbitrary selection.

Good **beaches** in the San Diego area can be found at Silver Strand, Mission and La Jolla. In Los Angeles the best beaches are Redondo, Hermosa, Manhattan, Venice, Santa Monica, Malibu and Zuma. One warning to **83** swimmers further north: at the lovely Carmel resort, the beach is great for sun-bathing but the sea's undercurrents are dangerous for swimming.

California **surfing** is second only to Hawaii's, the experts say (non-Australian experts) and the best waves are to be found at Malibu on Point Duma and Surfrider, at Santa Monica State Beach, north of the pier, and at La Jolla on Windansea and Boomer.

Good **snorkelling** is to be found at Abalone Cove on the Palos Verdes Peninsula south of L.A., at Corona del Mar near Newport Beach, and at La Jolla Cove. There is unfortunately, poor snorkelling at Malibu, but great **scuba diving** can be enjoyed among its kelp beds. At all these Southern California beaches you will also find **windsurfing** and **waterskiing,** the latter good, too, up north at Sausalito and Tiburon.

San Diego is the unchallenged leader in the state for the sheer variety of its **sailing.** Every conceivable kind of vessel from the smallest rowing boat to the largest ocean-going sloop can be seen somewhere around Mission Bay and around the man-made Shelter Island and Harbor Island in San Diego Bay. Bring your own, rent one or—it's been done—hitch a ride from the

dock. Long Beach's Alamitos Bay and Los Angeles Harbor's Cabrillo Beach are also major centres for sailing, but L.A.'s largest pleasure-boat harbour is Marina del Rey, with moorings for over 6,000 vessels in a year-round resort atmosphere. You can rent power and sailboats here to coast around the marina. Further north, you'll find good sailing at Monterey, Sausalito and Tiburon.

Deep-sea fishing is available from all of these sailing harbours.

Other Sports

If you're a **tennis** enthusiast, pack your racket. Public courts are cheap—just a few dollars an hour even in Beverly Hills (at Roxbury Park, 401 S. Roxbury Drive)—and they're everywhere. The best municipal courts, floodlit at night, are in San Francisco's Golden Gate Park, San Diego's Balboa, L.A.'s Griffith, but there are usually dozens within walking distance of your hotel; more often than not your hotel will have one.

Golf, too, is much cheaper than in Europe, with courses all around the major cities—L.A.'s Griffith Park, for instance, has two nine-hole courses, San Francisco's Golden Gate has one. But the golf capital of

California is undoubtedly the Monterey Peninsula, with eighteen 18-hole courses, half of them public, and others that make arrangements with your hotel if you're staying in the area. The best of the public courses are the Del Monte in Monterey, the Pebble Beach, Spyglass Hill in Pebble Beach, and the Rancho Canada in Carmel. There are also excellent golf courses (and many tournaments held) in Palm Springs.

The other great outdoor sport in this health- and fitness-crazy state is **jogging,** which you can do everywhere, best of all perhaps barefoot along the beaches. The sports stores will try to sell you all manner of "essential jogging equipment"—haute couture tracksuits and running shoes,

Wheels are such an important part of life in Los Angeles that the kids now grow them on their feet.

Swiss timers, sweatbands, pedo-meters. But all you really need is a good pair of shoes and a towel. The rest is not essential and even the towel you can borrow from your hotel.

Not exactly healthy, unless you enjoy nursing grazed knees and elbows, but still popular is **roller skating,** above all at Venice where you can rent skates right on the beach-front, and **skateboarding.**

Back Country Sports

Try **freshwater fishing** in the National Parks. Get yourself a California fishing licence and go on a camping expedition in Yosemite along the Tuolomne River or at Merced Lake, a three-day trip from Yosemite Valley. In Sequoia there are good fishing trips to be made from Bearpaw Meadow.

Yosemite and Sequoia are also great places for **horse-riding,** with rental stables near the main hotels and lodges. In the winter **cross-country skiing** is first-class around Yosemite Valley and its wild country and **down-hill skiing** at Badger Pass and in Squaw Valley near Lake Tahoe. Ask at the tourist office for the *Winter Sports Guide* for a full list of skiing resorts.

Mountain climbing is a real challenge on Yosemite's cliffs and the best possible way of get-ting away from the summer crowds.

Spectator Sports

The spectator sports are great fun here. If only for anthropolog-ical reasons, Europeans coming in winter should watch the excit-ing brutalities of **American foot-ball.** The San Diego Chargers and Los Angeles Rams both have large and faithful followings, but the San Francisco 49ers were consistently the most successful California team throughout the eighties, winning the U.S. Super-bowl championship three times in the decade.

At the college level, where the high spirits of the cheer-leaders and fans are much more fun, the team with the strongest tradi-tion is the Trojans of L.A.'s University of Southern Cali-fornia.

Major league **baseball** is also represented in San Francisco, Los Angeles (two teams) and San Diego, though you have to be a real aficionado to be able to sit through all nine innings; for a foreigner, unfamiliar with the sport, the ritual—hot dogs, funny hats and all—is worth at least an hour.

Basketball is played in both L.A. and San Francisco, at college and professional level. There's **horse** 87

racing at L.A.'s Santa Anita and Hollywood Park.

One other spectator sport—that appears to attract many more women than men—is the **weight-lifting** down at the beach park in Venice. If you feel your bi- and triceps are up to it, why not have a go at "pumping iron" yourself.

If you can't find anyone else to juggle with, try your mother, or, if you're a mother, try your son.

Nightlife

In this instance, San Francisco is much more fun than Los Angeles. Most people in L.A. seem to stay home in the evenings or at least to have their fun in private. But San Franciscans go out a lot and the coffee house and street life is booming and bouncing with vitality every night.

Bars in San Francisco are a whole way of life—downtown Irish bars on Geary, Italian coffee-houses and every other ethnic variety in North Beach, and a host of late-night waterfront "joints" along Embarcadero to Fisherman's Wharf. There's no obvious distinction to be made between "tourist traps" and local hang-outs, perhaps because San Franciscans are the most enthusiastic tourists in their own town, so you'll be mixing with the locals wherever you go. Some bar-cafés around North Beach specialize in very good amateur opera singing—you'll hear it as you walk by the open doors. If it sounds too much like Pavarotti or Callas, it probably is Pavarotti or Callas on the jukebox played between "sets".

Broadway is also the main thoroughfare for jazz **nightclubs** and "topless", "bottomless" and other forms of stripjoint, most of them more innocent than they seem, with signs inviting you merely to "see and talk to a live nude girl in your own private booth". The South of Market district, or SoMa, is home of a dynamic night-life scene, with clubs staying open until the sun comes up.

The few bars in Los Angeles are mostly around Hollywood, along Sunset Strip, or among the student community in Westwood and out in Santa Monica, plus some colourful singles bars along the harbour at Marina del Rey. Bars as places of work are a phenomenon of Beverly Hills, where the almighty "deal" is transacted among agents, producers, actors and directors in the lounges of the great hotels—the Regent-Beverly Wilshire, the Hilton and above all the Polo Lounge of the Beverly Hills Hotel on Sunset Boulevard. Watching the facial expressions is an entertainment all of its own.

The Los Angeles Philharmonic Orchestra perform excellent **concerts** at the Dorothy Chandler Pavilion in the Music Center and also in the open air at the Hollywood Bowl, "Symphonies under the Stars" in the summer season. You should look out for the recitals and concerts at Royce Hall on the campus of UCLA. The San Francisco Symphony performs from December to May at the Davies **89**

Hall and gives concerts of lighter music in the summer at the Civic Auditorium.

Opera and **ballet** also have their place in Californian nightlife. The San Francisco Opera is one of the best in the country and attracts leading international singers to its three-month season beginning in mid-September. The Curran Theatre holds Spring Opera in March for new American singers. The San Francisco Ballet has its major season at the Opera House in the spring, but also performs in December.

Theatre gets too much competition from the cinema in Los Angeles to reach a consistently high level, but there are occasionally good visiting companies at the Ahmanson Theatre and at the Shubert Theatre in Century City. San Francisco has a good repertory company, the American Conservatory Theater, performing a changing programme from October to May at the Geary Theater and one major production through the summer months.

Which brings us to **cinema**. In Los Angeles, home of the film industry, there are three yearly events: the American Film Institute sponsors an international film festival in April; a European film festival takes place in June; and there is a festival of comic films in September.

San Francisco's film festival runs from mid-April through early May, with showings at the Kabuki Cinemas in San Francisco and at the Pacific Film Archives in Berkeley. Both attract major international productions. The summit of cinematic folklore is reached in April when the Oscar awards ceremony is held at the Dorothy Chandler Pavilion. Admission is by invitation only, to members of the Motion Pictures Academy, nominees and their friends. If you're not one of them, you might still like to go along and join the crowds to watch the stars arrive. They still smile for the klieg-lights and cameras, turning up in the sunny afternoon in elaborate evening-wear.

For serious film-goers, the best cinemas in L.A. are around Westwood, but the great old palaces are up in Hollywood (see p. 58). Unlike in Europe, the summer months here are a season for major new releases that won't open overseas till the autumn or around Christmas time.

With **disco** faltering, California entrepreneurs are frantically looking for its replacement; but you still find it lingering on in a few plush locations in Beverly Hills and among the singles bars out at Marina del Rey and in the Los Angeles area.

Shopping

California has long been a trend-setter in casual clothes, gadgets, games and equipment for outdoor living, surfboards, roller-skates, skateboards, boogie boards (for bodysurfing in the ocean), basketball shoes, tents and the best skipping-ropes in the U.S. Most of the goods for sale in California are all available elsewhere, but you are more likely to find them here first.

There are open-air art fairs in all major cities, offering prints, posters, photos—even paintings.

San Francisco Area

The leading elegant shopping district centres on **Union Square,** with all the major New York and Californian department stores represented. There is a special emphasis on the classic tailoring of the more conservative clothing stores, like Brooks Brothers. The shopping centres of Ghirardelli Square and The Cannery at Fisherman's Wharf are aimed at the younger set. Both are situated in pleasant surroundings with open-air cafés, bookshops and restaurants.

Not forgetting that San Francisco was created by the

Gold Rush, you should plan to bring home a pair of blue jeans, the revolutionary garb that clothed the miners, with rivets reinforcing the seams so that the pockets could hold gold nuggets without bursting. You're sure to find some in the Embarcadero shopping centre, known as Rockefeller West—a triple-level complex of shops, restaurants, sculpture courts, walkways and bridges that promises a full day of shopping. You might also consider buying here a ten-gallon cowboy hat; San Francisco claims to make the best.

North Beach is noteworthy above all for its bookstores. One of them, the City Lights Bookstore at Columbus and Pacific, an old beatnik mecca, is a local institution.

L.A. shopping ranges from Rodeo Drive chic to Bugs Bunny mania.

Los Angeles Area

In California, the major cities all have elegant shopping districts, but the most spectacular is **Rodeo Drive** in Beverly Hills, Los Angeles. It seems that the world's most exclusive shops for leather goods, jewellry and other luxury articles have all opened up branches on Rodeo Drive. A little bit of Rome's Via Borghese, Paris's Rue du Faubourg St. Honoré and London's Bond Street have all found their way here. But L.A. has other elegant shopping districts: Wilshire Boulevard (ironically named after eccentric socialist Gaylord Wilshire) and Century City. Of the great department stores, I. Magnin's (formerly Bullock's) is a local institution, competing with branches of the major national stores—Saks Fifth Avenue, Neiman-Marcus and Nordstrom's.

T-shirts and jeans seem to be one fashion that won't die; they just change their colour or shape from time to time. New designs are likely to appear first in Hollywood on Melrose Avenue.

Hollywood, naturally enough, is the centre for cinema paraphernalia: original posters that have become collectors' items, pin-ups and film star masks. Along Hollywood Boulevard, you'll find collections of books on the film industry.

Flea markets are set up along the waterfront at Venice and, on Saturdays, at Pasadena's Rose Bowl. But you should also look out for the "garage sales" that are advertised in residential areas, where families clear out unwanted articles—everything from old tennis rackets to kitchen gadgets. This community of lightning obsolescence offers you some amazing bargains, as well as pieces of Americana that may mean more to foreigners than to other Americans.

Resort Shopping

All the seaside resorts along the coast have attractive boutiques, but the best are at Sausalito, Carmel, Newport Beach and La Jolla. At Pebble Beach, near the golf courses of the Monterey Peninsula, you will also find a magnificent collection of golf and other sports equipment.

Wining and Dining

The good things to eat in California are undoubtedly the simple things. And thanks to diversified agriculture, a blessed climate and the fisheries that line a long coastline, the fruit, vegetables, meat and fish produced here are fresher, and usually larger, than almost anywhere else in the United States.

Where to Eat

There are a variety of different places where you can enjoy the delicious food. Dine in the luxurious surroundings of a trendy Chinese restaurant or eat a simple meal under the California stars. Take away the makings of a picnic lunch from one of the well-stocked delicatessens or feast on Mexican-American specialities.

Some restaurants provide valet parking for your car—a great convenience where parking spaces are few and far between. Drive up to the entrance and leave your car with an attendant, who will give you a numbered ticket. You usually pay a small fee.

Many restaurants charge more for dinner than for lunch. In simple eating houses, you often pay the cashier on your way out, after leaving a tip on the table.

Meal Times

Many restaurants are open at all hours of the day and night. Breakfast is usually available from 7 to 10 a.m., though British visitors may be surprised to find that some restaurants continue to serve pancakes, waffles and egg dishes throughout the day. Lunch hour extends from 11 a.m. to 2.30 p.m. and dinner is served from 5.30 to 10.30 p.m. or thereabouts.

Eating Habits

For Europeans, Californian eating habits may need some introduction. As soon as you sit down for breakfast, you're likely to see the waitress advancing on you armed with a pot of coffee. Serving coffee is a hospitable way of saying "good morning" and it takes firm, clear action to stop this automatic gesture if you don't want coffee immediately. The coffee is weak by European standards, but your cup will be refilled several times.

If you're having fried eggs, remember to specify "sunny side up" (cooked from below only) or "over, easy" (turned and cooked lightly on top). Toast may be white, whole wheat or rye.

At lunch and dinner, salad is served before the main dish, which used to upset habitués of French cuisine; now, in these slimmer times of diets and health-foods, the salad makes a good appetizer. Salad dressings are often surprising concoctions not familiar to every European palate. If you want a simple dressing you can always order oil, vinegar and a little mustard and mix your own vinaigrette. America is not just the home of the brave, it's also the land of the free.

You may find that you are offered a cocktail before, during and after the meal: cocktails are not necessarily considered apéritifs. Alternatively, you can order wine immediately.

Specialities

Salads are a great favourite in the clean-living state of California. One of the best is raw spinach with a little sour cream and crisp crumbs of bacon. Avocados are another favourite, whether vinaigrette or filled with sea-food. Each chef claims his own secret for making Caesar's salad, which for purists is long-leafed romaine lettuce, hard-boiled eggs, garlic, olive oil and lemon juice.

Sea-food is especially good in San Francisco and Monterey, and around the San Diego Bay. You will come across superb sea bass, swordfish, tuna and the delicious long-fin tunny (tuna) known as albacore. This fresh seafood is at its best when prepared simply—steamed or grilled with a lemon-butter sauce.

While Boston makes its shellfish soups or chowders from clams, San Francisco has equally tasty abalone (also eaten raw) and oysters. Some San Francisco restaurants serve a dish called Hangtown Fry, an omelette made with ham and oysters. It is said to have been requested as a last breakfast by a gourmet criminal convicted of murder during the Gold Rush. There are some who feel he should have been hanged just for imagining such a dish, but others love it.

Crab is a great delicacy on the West Coast, whether amandine (salted and peppered in hot butter and Worcestershire sauce with sliced almonds) or broiled with parsley, chives and paprika. Crab Louis, a salad of crab meat, hard-boiled eggs, lettuce and tomatoes is served with a dressing of mayonnaise, chili sauce and horse-radish. (Connoisseurs insist on capers, too.) Jumbo shrimp, close relatives of the Mediterranean gamba, are wonderful barbecued in the shell with black pepper.

The best bet among **meat dishes** remains beef: steaks in an endless variety of cuts—Porterhouse, T-bone, sirloin, filet mignon, strip. Roast prime ribs of beef, a marvellous luxury, are served with a huge baked Idaho potato. Barbecued spare ribs

have a devoted following for both the beef and pork varieties. A little honey in the sauce makes all the difference.

Desserts in this state of year-round fresh fruit are a delight—strawberries, peaches, grapefruit, grapes, all a little larger and

Crabs, soft-shell or hard, from San Francisco's Fisherman's Wharf, are a delicacy for true gourmets.

Fast food may be quick to serve, but looking after its architecture is a lot of meticulous hard work.

try the strawberries thickly coated with chocolate that are served in some Beverly Hills establishments as an appetite-ruiner.

But above all, taste the ice-cream, natural dairy ice-cream in dozens of amazing flavours. You can make a whole meal of it in one of the many ice-cream parlours in Westwood. And don't miss that great national dish, apple pie, not at all a banal pleasure. Order it *à la mode,* with ice-cream on top.

Ethnic Cuisine's

American cooking is enriched, like the civilization itself, by ethnic diversity, and California has always been a mecca for foreign immigrants. Most of San Francisco's **Italians** didn't bother to stop off first in New York or Chicago, they went straight to the West Coast, and their restaurants in North Beach are among the best in the country. One Italian speciality is San Francisco's superb answer to bouillabaisse; a thick fish soup known as *cioppino,* more fish than soup, with every available shell-fish from the Pacific. It's spiced up or down, according to taste.

Similarly, the **Chinese** headed for California during and after the Gold Rush, and the rich abundance of local products made their cuisine as good as

sweeter than you remember eating elsewhere. Don't forget that California is rivalled only by Florida as the land of the orange. Demand it freshly squeezed, drink it by the gallon and you'll begin to look like a Californian. If, on the other hand, you'd like a **98** little decadence with your fruit,

you can find outside China. One of the special pleasures of visiting San Francisco's Chinatown, is sampling a *dim sum* smorgasbord of egg rolls, meat dumplings, deep-fried sweet potatoes and chopped mushrooms in wedges of rice-pastry, accompanied by pots of sauce. Enjoy your *dim sum* picnic in Washington Square; you can buy it at one of the Chinese groceries or delicatessens that line the way from Washington Street to Broadway.

The restaurants in and around Grant Avenue offer all the variations of Chinese regional cooking—Peking, Szechuan, Shanghai, as well as the Cantonese most familiar outside China. It's worth calling up a day in advance to order a whole Peking duck, glazed with honey and roasted slowly with spring onions. This gentle delicacy finds a sharp contrast in the spicy smoked duck you might try in a Szechuan or Hunan restaurant. But you mustn't overlook seafood, such as steamed sea bass prepared with chopped green onions, black beans, garlic, ginger and sesame oil or Szechuan shrimp, served piping hot in both senses of the word.

In recent years, Thai, Vietnamese and Japanese restaurants have been mushrooming all over California, too, adding new and exciting accents to the Asian food scene.

The best **Mexican** restaurants are to be found along La Cienega Boulevard in Los Angeles, and in San Diego. Like Chinatown's *dim sum* parlours, Mexican eating houses offer an array of food to take out—crispy *tacos,* moist *tostadas* and *tortillas* (cornmeal pancakes) stuffed with shredded beef or chicken, grated cheese, avocado and lettuce. But the best dishes are difficult to manage comfortably standing up. Stay in the restaurant and enjoy a meal of *sopa de mazorca con pollo* (chicken and corn soup), *carne de puerco en adobo* (pork in chili sauce) or *mole poblano* (chicken with almonds, sesame seeds, peanuts, chili, raisins and savoury chocolate sauce.)

The gastronomic favourite of Hollywood, **Jewish** delicatessens are situated on Fairfax Avenue and, for the most luxurious and elaborate, in Beverly Hills. For the uninitiated, Jewish food features Eastern European borscht, cabbage soups (red or green) with sour cream, gefilte fish and minced fish balls. Blintzes, a crisper version of the Russian blini, are folded over minced meat as an appetizer or sweet cream cheese as a dessert. Corned beef (salt-beef to the British) and spicy smoked Rumanian-style pastrami make **99** delicious sandwiches; they're served on rye bread with potato salad and pickled cucumbers. For dessert try cheese cake. It's such a classic that the Germans think it's German and the Americans think it's American. The Jews don't mind where it comes from, as long as it's thick and creamy, with the proper layer of sweet cake-crumb pastry underneath and some strawberries, blueberries or cherries on top.

One minority group's cuisine cuts across all ethnic lines, and that's **health food**—very popular in healthy California. There are lots of health food restaurants around Venice, Santa Monica and Mill Valley north of San Francisco. Every imaginable fruit and vegetable juice, plus delicious salads of all descriptions are served with a seraphic smile—and sometimes even a non-denominational benediction. As you take in all these vitamins, you can't help feeling a little morally superior—although you might tire of all the alfalfa.

Drinks

California is proud of its **wines** and for good reason. Wine-growers have refined and matured their techniques and improved the honesty of their marketing. In the old days, the wineries churn-ed out a mass production of red and white wines that they indiscriminately labelled "Burgundy" and "Chablis".

Now, with nationwide interest and taste for good wine increasing every year, as well as international appreciation, California wine-growers are taking more care.

Generally wines are distinguished by labels specifying the varieties of European grapes from which they were grown. The reds include *Cabernet Sauvignon* from the French Médoc, *Pinot Noir* from Burgundy and *Zinfandel,* whose origin puzzles the experts. Some believe it to be Italian, but you won't find it outside the state of California. The most important whites are *Chardonnay* from Burgundy, *Sauvignon Blanc* from Bordeaux, *Gewürztraminer* and *Riesling* from Alsace, the German Mosel and Rhineland. The vintage displayed on the labels of these wines represent the authentic year of at least 95% of the wine in the bottle.

All these improvements have meant an inevitable increase in price, but Californian wines now hold their own with many of the French, German and Italian. Although you'll perhaps find the best European vintages are still superior, but ordinary table wines are more often than not vastly inferior to their Californian counterparts.

Some of the local sparkling wines, too, have become world-class. In addition, there are vineyards where French producers such as Chandon are making their own Californian champagnes according to tried and true methods.

You can order wine by the glass or carafe, as well as by the bottle. If you go to a restaurant that doesn't have a liquor licence, it is perfectly acceptable to bring your own bottle of wine.

Wine may be the most popular drink in California, but there are alternatives. One of the more splendid Mexican gifts to America is **tequila,** best drunk in cocktail form as a Margarita—iced tequila with Cointreau or Triple Sec, lime juice and a coating of salt around the rim of the glass. Europeans will find that American **beers** are similar to English lager. Many foreign beers are served, too. You can always ask for a variety of fresh fruit juices or fizzy mineral water, the favourite of health-conscious Californians.

The finest scent in California is the bouquet of a Napa Valley wine.

California Round-Up

The majority of the most interesting and popular sights of California are
covered in this book. But, as in any other vast area, there are bound to be
places to visit which have been omitted. On this page we gather some of
them together and present a brief summary of their attractions.

Columbia State Historic Park (Columbia, Sierra Nevada): Large area
of old Gold Rush town preserved. Saloons, hotels, bank, etc.

Devil's Postpile National Monument (Mammoth Lakes area in eastern
Sierra Nevada): Extraordinary sheer basalt columns caused by volcanic
and glacial action.

Exposition Park (Downtown Los Angeles): Contains Museum of
Science and Industry, and Natural History Museum. Both worth visiting.

Forest Lawn Memorial Park (Glendale, north-east Los Angeles):
Statuary, gardens, religious paintings and stained glass windows.

Lake Tahoe (north-east of San Francisco in Sierra Nevada): Beautiful,
blue lake set in romantic forest surroundings; gambling on Nevada shores.

Lassen Volcanic National Park (north-eastern California): Steaming
fumaroles, lava flows and boiling mud pools create an absorbing atmosphere for amateur volcanologists.

Los Angeles State Historic Park (Downtown Los Angeles): Contains
historic highlights of city; Olvera Street Mexican market is particularly
colourful.

Marriott's Great America (Santa Clara, south of San Francisco):
Amusement and theme park, hair-raising rides.

Missions: apart from those already mentioned, keep an eye open for the
brown historic landmark panels on the freeways. There are 21 mission stations throughout California.

Palm Springs (south-east of Los Angeles in Colorado Desert): resort
offers relaxation, golf; take Palm Springs Aerial Tramway for spectacular
views; visit palm trees of Palm Canyon.

Ports O'Call Village (Los Angeles Harbour): Shops, eating places,
streets create last-century atmosphere.

Sacramento: California's capital. See Sutter's Fort and the domed State
Capitol Building. Guided tours.

Solvang (between San Luis Obispo and Santa Barbara): Known as
"Little Denmark", town contains a cheerful Danish community. See also
Mission Santa Ines.

Southwest Museum (East Los Angeles): Specializes in art and artifacts

of native cultures from Alaska to South America.

BLUEPRINT for a Perfect Trip

How to Get There

Although the fares and conditions described below have all been carefully checked, it is advisable to consult a travel agent for the latest information on fares and other arrangements.

From Great Britain

BY AIR: The major carriers offer daily non-stop flights from Heathrow to both Los Angeles and San Francisco. Average direct flying time is 11 hours. Fares available include First Class, Economy, Super-APEX (Advance Purchase Excursion), Special Economy and Standby. Super-APEX must be booked 21 days before travel for a stay of 7 to 180 days. Children fly for two-thirds of the Super-APEX fare. Special Economy fares can be booked any time and offer plenty of flexibility. Standby fares are bookable only on the day of travel, minimum 2 hours prior to departure.

Some U.S. airlines offer travellers from abroad a discount on the cost of each internal flight, or flat-rate unlimited-travel tickets. You must buy these tickets before you arrive in the U.S.A. Visitors to the States may also purchase the train and bus passes mentioned below.

Charter Flights and Package Tours: Many operators advertise holidays featuring Los Angeles, San Francisco or both cities, with excursions to Las Vegas, Yosemite, the Grand Canyon, etc. Fly-drive packages can be arranged through tour operators or certain airlines.

From North America

BY AIR: Direct flights connect over 100 American and Canadian cities to Los Angeles and San Francisco every day. As these routes are highly competitive, special fares are readily available and prices change frequently. The Super Saver fare must be booked and paid for 30 days in advance. Children fly for two-thirds of this fare. Most airlines sell round-trip Excursion tickets, requiring payment at least seven days before travel. Fly-drive vacations, including flight, hotel and rental car, are offered by many airlines.

BY BUS: California destinations are served by Greyhound coach. Passengers can make as many stopovers en route as they choose, provided the destination is reached before the ticket expires. Both companies offer flat-rate rover passes for specified periods of unlimited travel. These tickets must be purchased outside the U.S. Sightseeing coach tours, including accommodation, are also available.

BY TRAIN: Los Angeles and San Francisco are linked to most of the major cities in the U.S.A. and Canada by Amtrak rail. Reductions are given on some popular routes, such as Chicago/Los Angeles. Amtrak offers a variety of bargain fares, including Excursion and Family fares, USA Rail Passes and tour packages with hotel and guide included.

BY CAR: The excellent Interstate freeway system criss-crosses the entire U.S.A. Odd numbers designate freeways running north-south, while even-numbered interstates run east-west. Interstate 80, for example, links New York with San Francisco, Interstate 5 goes from Vancouver to San Diego.

When to Go

The average temperatures of southern and northern California differ. Los Angeles enjoys a warmer, Mediterranean-like climate year-round, while San Francisco has more rainfall and sudden cool fogs on occasion. August, September and October are the warmest months in San Francisco, with temperatures often reaching the 80s; wettest months are December through February.

Monthly average maximum daytime temperatures:

		J	F	M	A	M	J	J	A	S	O	N	D
Los Angeles	°C	18	19	20	22	23	25	28	29	28	25	23	19
	°F	64	66	68	72	74	77	82	84	82	77	74	66
San Francisco	°C	13	15	16	17	17	18	18	18	20	20	18	14
	°F	55	59	61	63	63	64	64	64	68	68	64	57

Planning Your Budget

To give you an idea of what to expect, here's a list of prices in U.S. dollars. They can only be regarded as *approximate,* however, as inflation pushes the cost of living ever higher.

Airport transfers. To Los Angeles by Airport Shuttle bus $10, by taxi $25. To San Francisco by airport bus $7, by taxi $25.

Babysitters. $4 per hour, plus transport expenses.

Bicycle hire. $5 per hour, $21 per day, $100 per week, plus deposit.

Camping. Entry fee $5 per vehicle, reservation fee $4, trail camps (hikers) $7 per night, developed campsites $14-16 per night, primitive sites $7 per night, trailer and camper hookups $16-24 per night.

Car hire. Rates vary considerably with the company, the location and the season. By way of comparison, here is the price of an economy car (e.g. Chevrolet Chevette) with unlimited mileage during high season: $30 per day, $200 per week.

Cigarettes (per packet of 20). American brands $2.20 and up; higher for foreign brands.

Entertainment. Cinema $7, nightclub $10 and up for cover charges, $4 for drinks, discotheques similar to nightclubs in price or free.

Hairdressers. *Woman's* haircut $15 and up, shampoo and set or blowdry $18 and up, colour rinse $45 and up. *Man's* haircut $10 and up.

Hotels (double room with bath). Budget or motel $70, moderate $95, de luxe from $130 and up.

Meals and drinks. Full breakfast $7, lunch in coffee shop $7, in restaurant $11, dinner from $15, coffee $1, soft drink $1, bottle of wine from $9, glass of beer $2, whisky $5.

Sightseeing. Museums up to $6, amusement parks $20 and up, San Francisco nightclub tour (with dinner) approx. $40 and up.

Youth hostels (per night). $12.

An A-Z Summary of
Practical Information and Facts

Certain items of information in this section may already be familiar to U.S. residents, but have veen included to be of help to visitors from overseas.

AIRPORTS

Los Angeles is served by Los Angeles International Airport (LAX) and **A** Burbank Airport. All international and most domestic flights land at LAX, with Burbank Airport duplicating some of the short-hop flights. At Los Angeles International you'll find currency-exchange offices, snack bars, car-hire agencies and duty-free shops.

A LAX passenger service called Super Shuttle provides pick-up and delivery to and from points throughout Los Angeles. The service—using eight-passenger vans—operates 24 hours. For information, ring 338-1111. Flight Line Shuttle (971-8268) also links Los Angeles International with hotels downtown.

A LAX-Burbank Airport service is provided by Valley Airport Shuttle (419-4000).

The regular RTD (Southern California Rapid Transit District) public bus service is less expensive.

Taxis can be found at taxi stands outside each LAX terminal. The trip into town takes approximately 30 minutes, longer during peak traffic hours. Your hotel might have a free limousine service for transportation into the city; inquire at the airport.

San Francisco is served by San Francisco International Airport (SFO), about 15 miles south of the city. The airport has currency-exchange offices, restaurants, cocktail lounges, car-hire agencies and duty-free shops.

Many hotels offer free limousine service into town. The limousines pick up hotel guests outside each terminal.

Taxis wait right outside the doors. The trip to the city centre takes anywhere from 20 to 40 minutes, depending on the traffic.

SFO Airporter provides frequent, non-stop coach travel between San Francisco International Airport, Union Square and the Financial Disctrict. Telephone 495-8404 for information.

A   A Super Shuttle service runs to and from the airport and any location in San Francisco. Because it provides practically a taxi service, but at a fixed—and lower—rate, the service has become increasingly popular. For details, ring 558-8500.

Domestic flights. Air travel is by far the quickest and most convenient way of getting around the U.S. The most-travelled routes have shuttle services, where no advance booking is required. Travellers from abroad have a chance on most airlines of getting a *Visit U.S.A.* ticket, which provides discounts and sets no fixed programme. To benefit from these reduced-price tickets, you must buy them before you arrive in the U.S.A. (or within 15 days of arrival).

C   **CAMPING.** There are regional, state and national parks in California. If you are a family touring several parks during your stay, inquire into the special rates available.

The state park system is extensive and ranges from recreation spots such as beaches and wayside campgrounds to reserves and wilderness areas. Among the more famous national parks are Yosemite and Sequoia/Kings Canyon. Accommodation in the most popular parks must be booked with the individual lodge itself, anywhere from four months to a year in advance, depending on the season. If you are backpacking overnight, you must obtain a permit from the park.

Campsites are divided into two categories: developed (usually including showers, piped drinking water, picnic tables and trailer hookups) or primitive (which ordinarily have only toilets and a central water supply). Camping on non-organized sites, unless on private property with the consent of the owner, is illegal in most places in California.

Although some campsites work on a first-come first-served basis, many require reservations at least eight weeks in advance. Reservations for state parks can be made by dialling MISTIX (800-444-7275) be prepared with the names and correct spelling of several campsites in the area you have chosen.

For more information on California **state parks**, contact:
California Department of Parks and Recreation, Publications Dpt.,P.O. Box 942896, Sacramento CAA 94296; general information tel. (916) 653-6995

For information on **national parks**, contact:
National Park Service, Building 201, Fort Mason, San Francisco, CA 94123, tel. (415) 556-0160

CAR HIRE and DRIVING. California is the land of rent-a-car and you will find many international and local firms to choose from. If you are

counting pennies, be sure to shop around for the best deal. You may want
a specific car waiting for you at the airport upon your arrival; in that case,
make sure to arrange it before you leave home.

Most car-rental companies offer a choice of a per diem fee plus mileage
fee, or a flat rate that includes unlimited mileage. If you are planning to
drive more than 70 miles a day, the latter is probably for you. You may
also want to look into rent-it-here, leave-it-there deals. All prices include
basic liability insurance.

A major credit card is essential to avoid paying a huge deposit. You
must also have a valid driver's licence and a passport. For tourists from
non-English-speaking countries, a translation of the driving licence is
highly recommended, together with the national licence itself, or failing
this, an International Driving Permit. If you are under 21 and wish to hire
a car, you must hold a major credit card in your own name.

On the road. Drive on the right and yield to any car coming from your
right unless otherwise indicated. In California you may make a right hand
turn at a red light, provided there is no cross-traffic and you have given
way to any pedestrians. Speed limits, almost always posted, are rather
strictly enforced. Beware of rain in Los Angeles; an oily film on streets
may cause cars to lose traction momentarily.

Highways (motorways). There are several terms used for different types
of highways. Toll highways are usually called turnpikes and high-speed
divided highways are called freeways or expressways. However, there are
no toll roads in California. You'll find toll stations at major bridges such
as Golden Gate Bridge and San Francisco–Oakland Bay Bridge.

Be well prepared before tackling California's extensive freeway system.
Map out your route ahead of time. Speed limits are clearly signposted.
Generally the limit on highways is 55 mph, but it goes up to 65 mph on
rural stretches of interstate highways in many states.

Gas (petrol) and services. Gas stations are numerous and easy to locate.
Many might be closed in the evenings and on weekends, particularly on
Sundays. At night, exact change or a credit card is required.

Parking. In the big cities, parking facilities consist mostly of meters and
parking lots or garages. If you park on the street, never leave your car next
to a fire hydrant, and be sure you obey the street signs or you might be
towed away—a costly proposition. In San Francisco, when parking on a
hill, make sure you turn your wheels into the curb or your car will be tick-
eted. Also, watch out for any signs warning that parking is prohibited
because of street cleaning.

C **Breakdowns and insurance.** If your car breaks down, either wait for a police car to come by or try to locate the nearest phone and call a local garage to tow you. If you are stopped on an Interstate freeway, there are call-boxes on the side of the road—just pick up the receiver and the Highway Patrol will answer.

Find out before you leave if your automobile insurance covers you away from home. California insurance companies offer short-term policies but at exorbitant rates. If you are renting a car, basic liability insurance is included, and you can pay extra for accident and collision coverage.

The American Automobile Association (AAA) can arrange short-term insurance for visiting owner-drivers. Contact AAA World Wide Travel:

1000 AAA Drive, Heathrow, Florida 32746-5603

Distances. Here are road distances in miles between some important centres, plus approximate hours of driving time:

San Diego–Anaheim	94	2 hr.
San Diego–Los Angeles	118	2 ½ hr.
Los Angeles–San Francisco	425	9 hr.
San Francisco–Yosemite National Park	193	41/2 hr.
Los Angeles–Sequoia National Park	227	5 hr.
Los Angeles–Las Vegas	284	6 hr.
Los Angeles–Tijuana, Mexico	135	2 ½ hr.

Road signs. In California you will encounter some international road signs, but you may see the following written signs as well:

U.S.	*British*
Detour	Diversion
Divided highway	Dual carriageway
Expressway	Motorway
No parking along highway	Clearway
Railroad crossing	Level crossing
Men working	Roadworks
Motorbike	Moped
No passing	No overtaking
Roadway	Carriageway
Traffic circle	Roundabout
Traffic lane	Carriageway
Yield	Give way

CHILDREN. California is a land of enchantment for children. At Marineland (Los Angeles area) they can swim with the fish; on Catalina Island between December and April they can watch the annual migration of the whales; at the Los Angeles and San Francisco Planetariums they can observe the stars.

The list of things to do, including beaches and parks, is endless. Most amusement parks have special sections for younger children, and at the Los Angeles and San Francisco Zoos they can pet and feed some of the animals. There are even escort services in the larger cities that take groups of children on guided tours.

CIGARETTES, CIGARS, TOBACCO. Buying American cigarettes over the counter at supermarkets and drugstores is cheaper than buying them from vending machines in restaurants and bars. For the widest selection of international cigarette brands and tobaccos, look in the classified section of the phone book under "Cigarette and Tobacco Dealers". The choice of cigars is very good, though Cuban makes are not available in the U.S.

Clearly marked signs prohibiting smoking are visible in a number of public places. In restaurants there are often smoking and no-smoking sections.

CLOTHING. If you are going solely to Los Angeles, forget about packing heavy coats and bulky jackets—you won't need them. Most people dress all year round in casual, comfortable, light-weight clothes. Women may want a silk dress or some dressy slacks if they are planning to dine in the fancier restaurants. Men might bring a tie, just in case. If you are travelling during the winter months, you may run into a day or two of rain, but a light jacket should be sufficient as temperatures remain fairly warm.

In San Francisco, clothing styles are dressier and more sophisticated than in Los Angeles, although the trend is towards individuality. Don't forget a good pair of walking shoes and make sure they're broken in before you set out. For the summer and autumn months, in addition to light-weight clothes, women should pack a knit dress and a warm sweater in case the temperature drops. From November through April, come prepared for rain and colder temperatures with a warm coat or a lined raincoat. Women should bring some woollen skirts and dresses. For men, a number of restaurants require jacket and tie in the evening.

COMMUNICATIONS

Post offices. The U.S. postal service deals only with mail. Post office hours are from 8 to 9 a.m. to 5 or 6 p.m. Monday to Friday, and from 8 or 9 a.m. to 12 noon or 1 p.m. on Saturday. Some branches have longer hours; all are closed on Sunday. Stamps can also be purchased from vending machines in drugstores, air, rail and bus terminals and other public **111**

C places. Stamps cost less, however, at the post office. U.S. mail boxes are blue and are located on street corners.

Poste restante (general delivery). If you don't know what your address will be and you want to receive mail, have it sent to you (in Los Angeles) care of General Delivery, Metropolitan Station, 901 South Broadway, Los Angeles, CA 90014 (they require advance notice), or (in San Francisco) care of General Delivery, Main Post Office, 7th and Mission, San Francisco, CA 94101. Your mail will be held for 30 days.

American Express will also hold mail for foreign visitors (without charge if you hold their traveller's cheques or credit card):

c/o American Express, 723 W. 7th Street, Los Angeles, CA 90017

c/o American Express, 237 Post, San Francisco, CA 94111

Telegrams, faxes and telex. In contrast to many European countries, telegraph services in the U.S. are privately run and are not affiliated with the post office. You can telephone a telegraph office (check the Yellow Pages), dictate the message and have the charge added to your hotel bill, or dictate it from a coin-operated phone and pay on the spot. A letter telegram (night letter) costs about half the rate of a normal telegram, but takes at least twice as long to arrive.

Most hotels are equipped to handle faxes, as are a number of firms such as copier companies. There is no public telex service in California. Telexes are sent as regular cable-wires, then delivered as telexes by the receiving country.

Telephone. Public telephones can be found in hotel lobbies, restaurants, drugstores, rail and air terminals, gas stations, sidewalk booths and along the highway. Directions for use are on the instrument.

Telephone rates are listed and explained in the front of the White Pages of the telephone directory. Also included is information on person-to-person (personal) calls, collect (reverse-charge) calls, conference, station-to-station and credit-card calls. All numbers with an 800 prefix are toll-free (no charge). There are reductions for phoning at night, on weekends and on holidays.

The telephone is part of the American private enterprise system, and is not connected with the post office, so do not plan on mailing your letters and placing an overseas call at the same time. Long-distance call charges are calculated per minute; direct-dialling is the easiest and fastest method even from a phone booth. After three minutes the operator will interrupt to

tell you to add more money. If you need assistance, dial "0" and ask for an
overseas operator.

COMPLAINTS. If you have a serious complaint about certain business practices, and have talked with the manager of the establishment in question without success, try calling the Consumer Complaint and Protection Coordinators at (213) 620-5225 in Los Angeles, or at 1 (800) 952-5548 (a toll-free number that can be called from anywhere in California) in San Francisco.

CONSULATES. If you plan to stay in the United States for more than a month you should register with your consulate. This will facilitate things in case you lose your passport, for example.

Consulates in Los Angeles:

Australia: 611 N. Larchmont Boulevard, tel. 469-4300;
    hours: 10 a.m. to 3 p.m., Monday to Friday.

Canada: 300 S. Grand Avenue, tel. 687-7432;
    hours: 9 a.m. to 4.30 p.m., Monday to Friday.

New Zealand: 10960 Wilshire Boulevard, tel. 477-8241;
    hours: 9 a.m. to 5 p.m., Monday to Friday.

South Africa: 50 N. La Cienega Boulevard, Beverly Hills, tel. 657-9200;
    hours: 8.15 a.m. to 12.30 p.m. and 1 to 4.30 p.m., Monday to Friday.

United Kingdom: 3701 Wilshire Boulevard, tel. 385-7381;
    hours: 9 a.m. to 5 p.m., Monday to Friday.

Consulates in San Francisco:

Australia: 1 Bush Street, 7th floor, tel. 362-6160;
    hours: 9 a.m. to 4 p.m., Monday to Friday.

Canada: 50 Fremont Street, tel. 495-6021;
    hours: 9 a.m. to 5 p.m., Monday to Friday.

Eire: 655 Montgomery Street, tel. 392-4214;
    hours: 9 a.m. to 4 p.m., Monday to Friday.

United Kingdom: 1 Sansome Street, tel. 981-3030;
    hours: 9 a.m. to 4p.m., Monday to Friday; closed 1-2 p.m. for lunch.

C **CRIME and THEFT.** Crime is on the rise in California, especially in the cities, so use common sense to protect yourself. Keep a close watch on your luggage at San Francisco's airport. Carry as little cash as possible—deposit the rest of your money and traveller's cheques, and any valuables you might have, in your hotel safe. Place any possessions you leave in your car under the seats or lock them in the trunk. If driving around, be particularly careful about parking in the Fisherman's Wharf area, a favourite spot for car break-ins. At night, avoid venturing out alone and stay away from poorly lit streets and seedy, run-down areas. If in doubt, discuss your plans with the hotel staff, who will be able to advise you.

CUSTOMS and ENTRY FORMALITIES. To enter the United States, foreign visitors need a valid passport and a visitor's visa, which can be obtained at any U.S. embassy or consulate. Canadians need only present proof of nationality. Everyone must fill out customs declaration forms before arrival (usually distributed by your airline near the end of the flight). If you need any assistance going through Immigration and Customs at the airport, call on the multi-lingual, red-jacketed personnel there to come to your aid.

The following chart shows certain duty-free items you may take into the U.S. (if you are over 21) and, when returning home, into your own country:

Into:	Cigarettes		Cigars		Tobacco	Spirits		Wine
U.S.A.	200	or	50	or	1,350 g.	1 l.	or	1 l.
Australia	200	or	250 g.	or	250 g.	1 l.	or	1 l.
Canada	200	and	50	and	900 g.	1.1 l.	or	1.1 l.
Eire	200	or	50	or	250 g.	1 l.	and	2 l.
N.Zealand	200	or	50	or	250 g.	1 l.	and	4.5 l.
S.Africa	400	and	50	and	250 g.	1 l.	and	2 l.
U.K.	200	or	50	or	250 g.	1 l.	and	2 l.

A non-resident may claim, free of duty and taxes, articles up to $100 in value for use as gifts for other persons. The exemption is valid only if the gifts accompany you, if you stay 72 hours or more and have not claimed this exemption within the preceding 6 months. Up to 100 cigars may be included within this gift exemption.

Plants and foodstuffs also are subject to strict control; visitors from abroad may not import fruits, vegetables or meat. The same goes for chocolates that contain liqueur.

Arriving and departing passengers should report any money or cheques, **C**
etc., exceeding a total of $10,000.

ELECTRIC CURRENT. 110-volt 60-cycle A.C. is standard throughout the U.S. Plugs are the flat, two-pronged variety. Visitors from abroad will need a transformer (240-110 V) and probably an adaptor plug for their electric razors.

EMERGENCIES. Because of its vast size, Los Angeles has several police and fire departments and ambulance services. In case of emergency it is best to dial "0" and the operator will connect you with the service you need. Follow this procedure anywhere in California if you need help. In Los Angeles as in San Francisco, dial 911 to connect with police, fire department, ambulance and paramedics.

GUIDES and TOURS. Your nearest Visitors Information Center can give **G**
you a list of agencies offering organized city tours. Tour buses are comfortable and air-conditioned, and have toilet facilities. Guided tours are conducted at some major attractions as part of the admission fee.

HAIRDRESSERS and BARBERS. The Yellow Pages of the telephone **H**
directory list a wide choice of beauty salons, many of which cater not only to women but also to men. For men there is also a listing under "Barbers". Call to make an appointment, and inquire about prices, as these vary enormously. Many hotels have their own beauty salon. Tipping is customary.

HEALTH and MEDICAL CARE. Before you leave home, you should make arrangements to obtain temporary health insurance through your travel agent or check whether your policy covers you abroad. The U.S. does not offer free medical service, and a trip to the doctor can prove to be quite an expense.

If you need a doctor, you may want your consulate's recommendation, or you can call the Los Angeles County Medical Association at (213) 483-6122 or the San Francisco Medical Society at (415) 561-0853. If you need a dentist, the Los Angeles Dental Society and the San Francisco Dental Society both run a 24-hour referral service. Dial 481-2133 in Los Angeles, 421-1435 in San Francisco.

A prescription is required in California for most medicines. It can be filled at any local pharmacy. Also known as drugstores, pharmacies are usually open seven days a week and many offer delivery service.

California tap water is potable and served by the best restaurants, unless you request bottled water. In areas where there is a shortage of water many restaurants serve water only when asked. Most brands of mineral water, **115**

H including many European brands, can be purchased at your local super-market.

HITCH-HIKING. It is legal to hitch-hike in California as long as you "thumb a ride" from a sidewalk. In other words, stay off freeways and on-ramps to freeways. Hitch-hiking, however, does not have the best reputation—one hears too many stories of assault and robbery. As a result, Californians, usually a warm-hearted lot, are wary of picking up anybody, and you may find yourself waiting hours for a ride.

HOTELS and ACCOMMODATION. To ensure the type of accommodation you want, it is best to make advance hotel reservations in Los Angeles and San Francisco, even if you are travelling during the off-season. You may want to inquire about weekly rates, weekend discounts and family schemes (no charge for children occupying the same room as their parents). Unless you are on a pre-paid tour, no meals will be included in the price of a room. Almost all rooms have adjoining bath, air-conditioning and television, and many hotels and motor hotels have swimming pools. Many hotels in Los Angeles and San Francisco offer reduced rates and full-board arrangements from Friday to Sunday to offset the drop in business travel bookings at the weekend. You can obtain a list of accommodation at the nearest Visitors Information Center. For information on lodging in California's parks, see under CAMPING.

Motels. Motor hotels or "motels" are one of America's great bargains. Many belong to national (or even international) chains, so you can make all the bookings for your trip at the same time, from San Diego to the Oregon border if you like. Another advantage—motels are often conveniently located on or near major highways.

Bed-and-Breakfast establishments are found in smaller towns and holiday centres. The California Office of Tourism publishes information on some 200 properties in the brochure *California Bed-and-Breakfast Inns*. There are an increasing number of bed-and-breakfast possibilities in San Francisco, some in elegantly restored Victorian houses. Ring Bed & Breakfast International (415-696-1690) for information and bookings.

Youth hostels. Unlike Europe, the U.S. is not well endowed with youth hostels. There are, nevertheless, 160-odd hostels scattered throughout the country. For further information, write to: American Youth Hostel Association, Inc., National Campus, Delaplane, VA 22025.

There are a number of residences run by the YMCA (Young Men's Christian Association) in Los Angeles and San Francisco and YWCA (Young Women's Christian Association) in San Francisco. Rates are quite reasonable, and you do not have to belong to the association to stay at the "Y".

HOURS. Retail stores are usually open from 9.30 or 10 a.m. to 5.30 or 6 p.m., Monday to Saturday. Most large stores, particularly department stores, stay open at least one night a week until 9 p.m. and some are open Sunday afternoons. Many supermarkets stay open 24 hours, 7 days a week. If you aren't near a supermarket, there are quite a few mini-markets which never close. Stores in the growing number of shopping malls are usually open late seven days a week.

San Francisco area sightseeing

Alcatraz. 9 a.m.–3 p.m. daily, till 5 p.m. in summer.

Coit Tower. 9 a.m.–4.30 p.m. daily.

Golden Gate Park. Museums 10 a.m.–5 p.m. Wednesday–Sunday. California Academy of Sciences 10 a.m.–5 p.m. daily, later in summer. Japanese Tea Garden 8 a.m. to sundown daily.

Palace of the Legion of Honor. Closed until mid-1990s, but normally open 10 a.m.–5 p.m. daily.

Palace of Fine Arts. 10 a.m.–5 p.m. Tuesday–Sunday (till 9.30 p.m. Wednesday).

Presidio. Fort Point National Historic Site 10 a.m.–5 p.m. daily except Christmas Day. Presidio Army Museum 10 a.m.–4 p.m. Tuesday–Sunday.

Los Angeles area sightseeing

ABC Television Network. 9 a.m.–5 p.m., Monday–Friday.

Burbank Studios. Tours at 10 a.m. and 2 p.m., Monday–Friday by reservation only.

Catalina. Boats leave from Long Beach and San Pedro all day in summer (June–September); less frequent departures in winter (reserve in advance). Daily flights from Long Beach and San Pedro Airports. 117

H *Disneyland.* All attractions are open from 10 a.m. to 6 p.m., Wednesday to Friday, and from 9 a.m. to 7 p.m. on Saturday and Sunday in winter. Open 9 a.m. to midnight daily in summer.

Farmers' Market. 9 a.m.–6.30 p.m., Monday–Saturday.

Huntington Library. 1–4.30 p.m. Tuesday–Sunday. Parking reservations required on Sundays.

J. Paul Getty Museum. 10 a.m.–5 p.m. Monday–Friday in summer, same hours Tuesday–Sunday in winter. Parking reservations required one week in advance, or take bus No. 434 from downtown LA.

Knott's Berry Farm. 10 a.m.–6 p.m. Monday, Tuesday and Friday; 10a.m.–10 p.m. Saturday and 10 a.m.–8 p.m. Sunday.

Movieland Wax Museum. 10 a.m.–9 p.m. Monday–Friday, 10 a.m.–11p.m. Saturday and Sunday.

NBC Studios. 8.30 a.m.–5 p.m. Monday–Friday, 10 a.m.–5 p.m. Saturday and Sunday.

Norton Simon Museum. 12 noon–6 p.m. Thursday–Sunday.

Queen Mary. 10 a.m.–3.30 p.m. daily in winter, 10 a.m.–4.30 p.m. daily in summer.

Universal Studios. 10 a.m.–3.30 p.m. Monday–Friday, 9.30 a.m.–4 p.m. Saturday and Sunday in winter; 8 a.m.–6 p.m. daily in summer.

L **LANGUAGE.** Californians think of themselves as not having an accent, though visitors from the British Isles or Australia may not agree. Certain words have different meanings for Americans and British. Here are a few which could be a source of confusion:

U.S.	*British*
admission	entry fee
bathroom	toilet (private)
bill	note (money)
billfold	wallet
check	bill (restaurant)
collect call	reverse charges
elevator	lift
first floor	ground floor
gasoline	petrol
liquor	spirits
liquor store	off-licence

pavement	road surface
purse/	handbag
pocketbook	
rest room	toilet (public)
round-trip	return (ticket)
second floor	first floor
sidewalk	pavement
stand in line	queue up
subway	underground
trailer	caravan
underpass	subway

LAUNDRY and DRY-CLEANING. Your hotel may offer a dry-cleaning and laundry service, but it will usually cost you less to seek out a local establishment (look in the classified pages of the phone book under "Cleaners"). Most dry-cleaners are open every day except Sunday, and many offer same-day or even one-hour service.

Launderettes (laundromats), consisting of coin-operated washing-machines and dryers, are very popular in the U.S. Look under "Laundries—Self Service" in the Yellow Pages. However, some laundromats may be in dubious areas, so check first.

LIQUOR REGULATIONS. In California, a special licence is required in order to sell alcoholic beverages (except beer), and not all supermarkets are licensed. To be sure of finding what you want, head for a liquor store. There are several strictly enforced liquor laws. The sale of alcohol is prohibited after 2 a.m., and as a result, nightlife shuts down at that hour. Carrying open bottles of liquor in your car is illegal.

The minimum age for purchasing or drinking any alcoholic beverage is 21. You might be asked to prove your age by showing some identification (called "I.D.").

LOST PROPERTY. Air, rail and bus terminals and many stores have special "lost-and-found" areas. Restaurants put aside lost articles in the hope that someone will claim them. If your lost property is valuable, contact the police. If you lose your passport, get in touch with your consulate immediately.

MAPS. You will find free maps and brochures in any tourist information office. City and state maps can be purchased in some bookstores and many petrol (gas) stations.

M **MEETING PEOPLE.** Americans are generally friendly, outgoing and curious, so don't be surprised if you are asked intimate questions five minutes after you've been introduced.

In San Francisco you should have no trouble meeting Americans, whether at the outdoor cafés, the coffee houses, Ghirardelli Square or Fisherman's Wharf. Los Angeles, being so spread out, presents more of a problem. The beach is always a good people-meeting spot, as well as the many discos.

For something more organized, San Francisco has an International Hospitality Center whose aim is to further international friendship by arranging for foreigners to visit in American homes. In Los Angeles, International Friends offers, for a price, to transport you to a dinner and evening with an American family. International Spare Room is in touch with people all over the United States willing to rent a room or rooms in their homes (for one to three weeks) to foreigners. Advance reservations and deposit are required.

International Visitors Center, 312 Sutter Street, Los Angeles, tel. (415) 986-1388

California Houseguest International Inc., 6051 Lindley Avenue, #6, Tarzana, CA 91356, tel. (818) 344-7878

International Spare Room, P.O. Box 518, Solana Beach, CA 92075, tel. (619) 755-3194

MONEY MATTERS

Currency. The dollar ($) is divided into 100 cents (¢).

Banknotes: $1, $2 (rare), $5, $10, $20, $50 and $100. Larger denominations are not in general circulation. All notes are the same size and same green colour, so be sure to double-check your cash before you spend it.

Coins: 1¢ (called penny), 5¢ (nickel), 10¢ (dime), 25¢ (quarter), 50¢ (half dollar) and $1. These coins are all round but have different circumferences.

Banks and currency exchange. Banks are traditionally open from 10a.m. to 3 p.m. Monday to Thursday, and from 10 a.m. to 6 p.m. on Friday. Larger ones will change foreign money and foreign-currency traveller's cheques.

In San Francisco, Macy's California (the department store) runs a currency exchange from 9.30 a.m. to 9 p.m. on weekdays, 9.30 a.m. to 6 p.m. on Saturday and 12 noon to 5 p.m. on Sunday.

Airports have foreign currency-exchange offices open quite late.

Credit cards. In California, credit cards are a way of life. The major ones are accepted as cash almost everywhere. They are also a widely used means of identification. However, when you "charge" with a credit card, you will have to produce a passport or other identification.

Traveller's cheques. Traveller's cheques in American dollars pose no problem, but if you have traveller's cheques in foreign currency, you'll have to go to a major bank to get them cashed. Be sure to keep, separately from the cheques themselves, your purchaser's receipt and a listing by serial number of the cheques, as these will be necessary to get a refund in case of loss or theft.

Prices. The price marked on an item never includes the California state sales tax of 8.25%, which is added to your bill at the cash register. The U.S. has a larger spread of prices for the same kind of item than you will find anywhere else, as well as a greater choice. The best prices are usually offered by huge discount houses, located just off the highways and in suburban areas. Independent service stations are cheaper than those run by the large oil companies.

NEWSPAPERS and MAGAZINES. The *San Francisco Chronicle* and the *San Francisco Examiner* are that city's main newspapers. They can be bought at drugstores, tobacconists' and from vending machines. The Sunday "Datebook" section carries detailed listings of what's going on in town.

The *Los Angeles Times* is the main L.A. newspaper, available on any news-stand. The *Times'* Sunday "Calendar" section offers extensive coverage of city happenings.

Most hotels give out a free local magazine full of facts and figures on lodging, dining and entertainment.

OUTDOOR RECREATION. In Los Angeles there are some great bicy- cling areas around the Westwood UCLA campus, in Griffith Park and along the beach. The Santa Monica and Venice beach fronts have several locations where you can hire bicycles. The Venice Promenade is a favourite with roller-skaters, and there are a number of places to rent from. Beware of skating on the bike path as it is forbidden and could earn you a fine. Fishing and sailing boats can be hired at Marina del Rey, Los Angeles' largest pleasure-boat harbour.

The hills of San Francisco are not conducive to bicycling, but Golden Gate Park has several good bike trails. Several bicycle hire shops can be found in Stanyan Street, on the park's eastern border. If you're headed for the park, you might also want to look into horseback riding—there are a

O number of equestrian trails that wind through the greenery. You can rent a horse, or a boat for a sail on Stowe Lake, right in the park.

Large sporting goods stores hire out camping equipment, including tents, by the day or week.

P **PETS.** If you are coming from abroad, don't bring your dog along. Laws in Great Britain, Eire, Australia and New Zealand are so strict that taking your pet back home may be very difficult or even impossible (as in Australia).

Dogs are usually barred from beaches, restaurants, foodshops and public transport. Be sure to ask ahead of time if your hotel allows animals.

A list of veterinarians can be found in the Yellow Pages.

PHOTOGRAPHY. Camera buffs won't want to miss the famous panoramic view from the top of Mulholland Drive in Los Angeles, but pick a fairly smog-free day. In San Francisco, the view from Coit Tower sweeps 360° out over the bay to the city itself and further inland. From the other side of the Golden Gate Bridge, you can capture a breathtaking view of the city from a distance. There's also a quite spectacular view from Twin Peaks, situated in the centre of San Francisco.

All well-known brands of film are easily found in airports, drugstores, camera shops or the photo service booths you'll find in parking lots, shopping centres, etc. Prices vary, so you may want to check out by telephone several photo supply and processing shops (see "Photo Finishing—Retail" in the Yellow Pages of the phone book). Film processing usually takes two to three days, but there are a number of one hour services for colour prints.

POLICE. You may have to look hard to find a policeman; they sometimes seem to be hiding. If you see one, he (and, increasingly, she) will most probably be in blue, wearing a badge and carrying a gun. In Golden Gate Park in San Francisco, he might well be on horseback. On the highways, police ride motorcycles or travel in patrol cars, usually black and white. Do not hesitate to approach any policeman and ask for assistance or information; helping you is part of their job. In case of emergency, find a phone, dial "0" and ask the operator to contact the police.

PUBLIC HOLIDAYS. Banks, post offices and most stores close on the following Monday if certain holidays (such as Christmas) are on Sunday. They close on Friday if those holidays fall on Saturday.

New Year's Day	January 1
Martin Luther King Day	Third Monday in January
Lincoln's Birthday	February 12
Washington's Birthday	Third Monday in February
Memorial day	July 4
Labor day	First Monday in September
Columbus Day	Second Monday October
Veteran's Day	November 11
Thanksgiving	Fourth Thursday in November
Christmas	December 25

PUBLIC TRANSPORT. There is no viable public transport in Los Angeles. The existing bus systems can only inadequately deal with the city's great sprawling area. The majority of the buses, operating mostly in the denser parts of the city, are run by RTD (Southern California Rapid Transit District). For information dial 626-4455, or look in the Yellow Pages of the telephone directory for the nearest RTD office.

Santa Monica Municipal Bus Lines service the West Los Angeles, Pacific Palisades and Marina del Rey areas. (Call 451-5445.)

Public transport in San Francisco consists of buses, streetcars, cable cars, ferries and the BART subway (see below). The buses and streetcars are run by MUNI (Municipal Railways) and serve the entire metropolitan area. For information, call 673-MUNI or pick up route maps at City Hall.

There are inter-city bus services to the communities outside San Francisco. A/C Transit (tel. 839-2882) covers the East Bay Area, Sam Trans (tel. 800-660-4BUS) covers the Bay Area to Palo Alto, and Golden Gate Transit (tel. 332-6600) covers Marin and Sonoma Counties via the Golden Gate Bridge.

Ferries depart daily from Fisherman's Wharf to Tiburon, Alcatraz and Angel Island (tel. 546-BOAT for information), and from the Ferry Building for Sausalito (tel. 332-6600).

Subway (underground). While Los Angeles has not yet committed itself to a subway, San Francisco has in recent years developed BART (Bay Area Rapid Transit System) linking 8 San Francisco stations with 25 East Bay terminals. The trains run frequently, from 4 a.m. to midnight Monday to Friday, 6 a.m. to midnight Saturday, and from 8 a.m. to midnight on Sunday. Route maps are located in the stations and on the trains. Tickets are bought from a coin-operated machine. You can buy an excursion ticket if you plan to enter and leave the network at the same station. For information, dial 788-BART.

R RADIO and TELEVISION. You'll almost certainly have radio and television in your hotel room, with a vast choice of programmes. Some television networks broadcast from 6 a.m. until around 3 or 4 the next morning, others never go off the air. The major networks are on channels 2, 4 and 7 in Los Angeles, and 4, 5 and 7 in San Francisco. Channel 28 in Los Angeles and channel 9 in San Francisco are run by the Public Broadcasting Service (PBS), offering fine programming without commercials. A variety of special-interest shows and foreign-language programmes are aired on cable networks.

RELIGIOUS SERVICES. California democratically harbours every conceivable religion and sect. For a list of churches, contact the tourist information office or look in the classified pages of the phone book. Saturday newspapers often list services for the following day.

T TAXIS. In Los Angeles, there are taxis lined up at the airports and major hotels, but do not expect to flag one down in the street; you won't find any. To telephone for a taxi, look in the Yellow Pages of the telephone directory for your area under "Taxicabs". There are several companies and rates vary slightly. Service is usually quite prompt, but because of Los Angeles distances, can be prohibitively expensive. Some companies accept credit cards if you ask in advance.

In San Francisco you can hail a cab in the street without much effort, as long as you're not in a residential part of town. If you telephone for a taxi you shouldn't have to wait more than ten minutes.

Fares are clearly marked along with the name and number of the driver (in case of complaints). A tip of at least 15% is expected. If you are taking a taxi from the airport into town, be sure you have several small banknotes, as taxis will not make change for large denominations.

TICKETS. Through BASS, which has outlets in all major department stores, you can buy tickets for many special events, theatre productions and sporting events, and make camping reservations for state and national parks and beaches. For BASS information in Los Angeles, call (213) 642-5700; in San Francisco, dial (415) TEL-ETIX for recorded calendar listings, (415) 762-2277 for credit card bookings. The San Francisco Downtown Center Box Office is located at 325 Mason and sells tickets to most of the current events (775-2021).

TIME and DATES. The continental United States is divided into four time zones; California is on Pacific Standard Time. In summer (between April and October) Daylight Savings Time is adopted and clocks are

moved ahead one hour. The following chart shows the time difference **T**
between California and various other locations in winter: To get the exact
time in Los Angeles, call 853-1212; in San Francisco, dial 767-8900.

In the U.S., as opposed to Europe, dates are written in the order
month/day/year; for example, 2/4/99 is February 4, 1999.

California	New York	London	Sydney
noon Sunday	3 p.m.. Sunday	8 p.m. Sunday	7 a.m. Monday

TIPPING. Service is usually not included on your restaurant or bar tab
and you are expected to tip your waiter, waitress or bartender 15% (more
if service is exceptional). However, several restaurants in San Francisco
have adopted the French practice of adding 15% to the bill as a service
charge. Doormen, bellhops and skycaps, etc., should also get a coin or two
for their services. Some suggestions:

Hotel Porter, per bag	50¢- $1 (minimum)
Hotel maid	$1 per day
Lavatory attendant	50¢
Taxi driver	15%
Tour guide	10-15% (optional)
Barber/hairdresser	15%

TOILETS. You should have no problem finding a toilet in California.
Facilities can be located in bus and railway terminals, in museums, large
stores, restaurants, airports, gas stations, and in most recreation areas. If
you encounter a pay-toilet, the usual charge is 10 cents.

Americans use the terms "restroom", "bathroom" and "ladies"or "men's
room" to indicate the toilet.

TOURIST INFORMATION OFFICES. Your local tourist information
centre should be able to assist you with any questions you might have.
Feel free to telephone, or drop by to pick up the Visitor and Convention
Guide and free brochures.

**San Francisco Visitor Information Center/Convention & Visitors
Bureau** 900 Market Street, Lower Level, Hallidie Plaza, tel. (415) 974-
6900. Dial (415) 391-2000 for information and 391-2001 for a recorded
summary of the day's events.

T **Los Angeles Visitor Information Center/Convention & Visitors Bureau** Arco Plaza, 515 S. Figueroa Street, tel. (213) 624-7300. There are also branches at 6541 Hollywood Blvd., Hollywood, tel. (213) 461-4213.

For information prior to arrival in the U.S., contact:
United States Travel Service, 22 Sackville Street, London W1; tel. (071) 439 7433

TRAINS. Amtrak is an inter-city rail passenger service which, in California, travels between San Diego, Los Angeles, Oakland and Berkeley. There are also connections from these points to Sacramento, Reno and cities to the east. For information and reservations call the toll-free (no charge) number below. The Los Angeles/San Francisco train leaves every morning from Union Station (800 North Alameda) and arrives in the evening at Oakland Amtrak Depot (16th Street). An Amtrak bus then takes you to the Passenger Service Center at 425 Mission in San Francisco.

The Southern Pacific Commuter Service runs trains daily from San Francisco to San José and peninsula cities in-between. The Southern Pacific Depot is located at 4th and Townsend in San Francisco, tel. (415) 557-8661. A bus service links this depot with the Amtrak Passenger Service Center.

Amtrak information and reservations, tel. (800) USA-RAIL (872-7245 in digits).

W **WEIGHTS and MEASURES.** The United States is one of the last countries in the world to change to the metric system, and is not yet involved in an official changeover programme. Some British visitors will be happy to go back to the "good old days" of feet and inches.

Milk and fruit juice can be bought by the quart or the half-gallon, but wine and spirits now come in litre bottles. Food products usually have the weight marked in ounces and pounds as well as in grams.

Index

An asterisk (*) next to a page number indicates a map reference. For index to Practical Information, see inside front cover.

128